GERALD & LEE
DURRELL
IN RUSSIA

GERALD & LEE DURRELL
IN RUSSIA

SIMON AND SCHUSTER NEW YORK

This book is for

JOHN HARTLEY

our friend and long-suffering
personal assistant, without
whose hard work, tact and
cheerfulness we would not have
achieved as much as we did
during our fascinating travels,
with great affection.

PICTURE CREDITS

Arakcheyer 123 *tl*, 123 *tr* Baturin 124 R. Charters 12 *inset*, 12-13, 16, 18, 20, 21, 27 *t*, 27 *bl*, 31 *bl*, 31 *tr*, 32 *r*, 37 *t*, 40 *r*, 44-45, 48 *bl*, 50 *fr*, 50 *l*, 51, 55 *b*, 56 *b*, 57 *cl*, 57 *b*, 57 *tr*, 59 *c*, 59 *br*, 65, 82 *tr*, 83 *cr*, 86 *tr*, 97 *t*, 97 *r*, 104-5, 107 *tl*, 108 *t*, 108 *br*, 110 *inset*, 110-111, 114 *t*, 116, 121 (*all*), 122 *t*, 125, 129 *tr*, 130, 131 *t*, 133 *l*, 133 *r*, 142, 143 *l*, 143 *tr*, 143 *br*, 146, 147 *t*, 147 *b*, 155, 161 *b*, 162 *inset l*, 164, 165 *b*, 166 *t*, 166 *b*, 167, 167 *tr*, 167 *l*, 169-171, 172 *t*, 173, 174 *t*, 174, 176 *br*, 177 *br*, 178, 179 *tl*, 179 *tr*, 180-181 *t*, 181 *b*, 189 *t*, 189 *b*, 190 Bruce Coleman 14, 66 *t*, 76 *inset*, 108 *bl*, 180 Debabov 71 Lee Durrell 33 *tl*, 70-1, 75, 108 *inset t* Friedburg 144 *inset*, 156 *tl* V. Gippenveyter 25 *br* Goloranova 83 *bc* Grazhdankin 57 *tl*, 104/2, 135 *t*, 141 *bl*, 141 J. Hartley 1, 18, 19, 22-23, 23 *inset*, 26 *tr*, 28, 29, 30, 33 *tr*, 33 *cr*, 36, 38, 39 *tl*, 39 *br*, 40-41, 40 *cl*, 47, 48 *tl*, 50 *r*, 50 *cr*, 50-51, 53, 59 *cr*, 60-61, 62-63, 64, 66 *b*, 68, 69, 70 *l*, 70 *c*, 72, 73 *tr*, 73 *bl*, 74 *inset*, 83 *cl*, 85 *l*, 85 *r*, 86 *cr*, 87 *tl*, 92 *t*, 93, 94-5, 94 *inset*, 98 *l*, 101, 102 *t*, 104 *t*, 104/4, 107, 108 *inset c*, 114 *b*, 115, 117 *b*, 120, 123 *c*, 126-7, 126 *inset*, 128, 132 *tr*, 132 *b*, 132 *cl*, 135 *b*, 138 *r*, 141 *fl*, 141 *r*, 144-5, 149 *b*, 152-3, 152 *insets*, 153 *insets*, 154, 156 *tr*, 159 *t*, 159 *b*, 160 *tl*, 160 *tr*, 160 *b*, 161, 162-3, 167 *cr*, 167 *br*, 167 *cb*, 174 *r*, 177 *tr*, 177 *bl*, 179 *c*, 184, 185 *t*, 185 *b* Paul Lang 67 Mashkov 87 *b* F. Mukhin 37 *br*, 82 *c*, 90-91, 108 *cr*, 125 *inset* Nechayer 83 *br*, 141 *l* A.C. Nikolayevsky 52 Ogniov 122 *b* B. Patchett 6, 15, 16, 17, 24, 25 *tl*, 26 *tl*, 31, 32 *c*, 34, 34-35, 40 *tl*, 40 *bl*, 40 *br*, 43, 44 *inset*, 46, 49, 49 *l*, 52, 54 *l*, 54 *r*, 55 *t*, 55 *inset*, 56 *t*, 58, 59 *t*, 59 *cl*, 59 *bl*, 59 *tr*, 62 *inset*, 73 *tl*, 73 *br*, 74, 76, 77, 78-79, 78, 80, 81, 83 *t*, 83 *bl*, 84 *tl*, 84 *tr*, 85 *t*, 86 *cfr*, 87 *tr*, 87 *c*, 92 *b*, 97 *cl*, 99, 100, 102 *b*, 103 *t*, 103 *b*, 104/3, 108 *inset b*, 112, 113, 113 *inset*, 117 *c*, 118-119, 123 *b*, 129 *tl*, 129 *b*, 131 *r*, 132 *tl*, 132 *bl*, 133 *b*, 134, 136, 137, 138 *l*, 140 *t*, 140 *b*, 148, 149 *t*, 151, 156 *l*, 157 *t*, 157 *cl*, 157 *tr*, 158, 161 *c*, 162 *inset r*, 165 *t*, 172, 174 *l*, 176 *t*, 176 *r*, 176 *c*, 176 *bl*, 177 *tl*, 177 *ct*, 177 *c*, 182-3, 187, 188 R.T. Papikyan *Frontispiece*, 32 *b* A. Petriush 37 *bl* P. Romanov 48 *br*, 89, 96 Shenbrot 106 *l*, 106 *r* Siokin 82 *tl* G. Smirnov 25 *tr* Viesman 157 *b*

CONTENTS

A word in advance

A YEAR ago I was sitting in a hotel bedroom in Moscow at ten in the morning, being interviewed by a gentleman from that illustrious newspaper, *Pravda*, and sharing a bottle of vodka, which he had so thoughtfully brought with him. The temperature outside the hotel was well below zero and it was obviously not the time of the year that the average tourist would choose for a junket to the Soviet Union. So I was doing my best to explain our presence at this inimical time to the *Pravda* correspondent, who obviously thought that we were all mad.

For three years we had been negotiating with Gostelradio (the Russian equivalent of the BBC) and various ministries to obtain permission to visit the Soviet Union and make a series of thirteen half-hour programmes on the animal life of this vast country and its conservation. But there was more to it than that. We in the West know very little of life inside Russia. All we ever seem to see on our television screens is Red Square full of tanks and rows of grey-faced politicians who look as though *nyet* is their favourite word. Surely, I thought, there must be other Soviet citizens apart from these politicians — citizens who laughed and loved and worked in that enormous country. So, as well as the fascinating flora and fauna, as well as the almost overwhelming variety of countryside, we wanted to try to show these people, these other Russians, and what they were like. Given the magnitude of the task, I think we succeeded.

The reader might find the arrangement of stories in this book a bit puzzling. The reason is that we, our crew and our specialist cameraman spent nearly ten months in the Soviet Union, but at different times of the year, for we wanted to show the seasons. We travelled over 150,000 miles and filmed in nineteen different locations, some of which had never been visited before by Westerners. For those interested in figures, there were eight of us and we had ninety-five pieces of baggage between us, which consisted not only of film, cameras, recording machines and so on, but also of clothing ranging from down parkas, for temperatures well below zero, to shorts for the desert. Naturally, when you come to write up a trip as complex as this, the great difficulty is to avoid having to keep stopping and explaining to your reader why in one chapter you are talking about sub-zero temperatures and in the next you are complaining about the blistering heat.

Both Lee and I were to keep copious diaries of our travels. Lee's was to contain all the stern scientific stuff, and I was going to record sights, sounds, colours and scents. In writing this book, of course, I borrowed heavily from Lee's diary, and so I wanted her to be named as my co-author, although the book is written mainly from my point of view.

Our team comprised Lee and myself; John Hartley, my personal assistant; Paul, our director; Rodney, our cameraman, and Byron, his assistant; Donna, who was our producer; Alex, our associate producer and translator; Ingrid, who for part of the trip was our sound recordist; and Ao, who took over from Ingrid for the latter half of the trip. We were a sort of travelling United Nations in fact, for both Donna and Alex were half Russian and Ao was Latvian (although all hailing from Canada), Rodney was from New Zealand, Byron a Canadian born and bred as was Paul, John and I were English and Lee was American, while Ingrid came from Holland.

When I had explained all this to the *Pravda* correspondent, he looked exceedingly bewildered and I wondered what sort of story he was going to write. You may well have begun to feel as bewildered as he was, but I ask you to press on as our story does become less complex.

Moscow at that moment when the icy claws of winter were starting to enfold it was not the most magical place to be. Those man-made termitariums called capital cities anywhere in the world, a-rustle and a-bustle with thousands of human beings, have never appealed to me, so it was not surprising that my first impressions of Moscow at the onset of winter were not altogether happy. The streets and pavements were piled high with scabs of dirty grey and black snow, everyone looking so pinched and drab and forlorn as they hurried, bent sickle-like against the biting winds that roared between the massive, gloomy, dun-coloured apartment blocks. Moscow is a city of crows, hooded crows, handsome birds in their jet-black and silvery-pink livery. They are everywhere in their hundreds, strolling through the snow banks in search of goodness knows what delicacies, sitting in the leafless trees in groups, gossiping in their harsh voices or else in flocks wheeling in the wind like flakes of wood ash in between the buildings. How they find enough food to keep their legions alive in this snow-strangled city is a mystery.

Naturally, getting ourselves and our extraordinary baggage into Moscow in the first place was a Herculean task, but we were now forced to spend several days there in order to attend to the many brain-aching hurdles of bureaucracy that are inevitable on a trip of this sort and magnitude, so that we could make sure that everything was in order for our first sorties outside the city.

In between running from office to office and from embassy to embassy, we took some time off to try to film in the Kremlin. When we got to the entrance, the crew weighted down with cameras, tripods and recording gear, it was not altogether unexpected that we were an object of curiosity to the police. A polite young man approached us, wearing a smart grey uniform and on his head what appeared to be a large Persian cat, lying somnolent and supine. This, on closer inspection, turned out to be his elegant fur hat. When he understood who we were and what we were doing, he got very excited and swore that of all my fans in the Soviet Union he was the most devoted and insisted on wringing my hand and slapping me on the back. I felt that, in a country like Russia where they view foreigners with some suspicion, it was an excellent start to have at least one policeman on my side.

Here in the Kremlin, behind their ancient bastions of red brick, are the famous cathedrals and churches, many with golden domes of different sizes like some strange giant Christmas-tree decorations perched on top. Even under a leaden sky and with flurries of snow falling, they shone with an incredible ancient lustre. Outside the red walls, at one end of Red Square, squats St Basil's Cathedral, surely one of the most charming and extraordinary of architectural confections, with its five fat domes, each candy-striped in bright primary colours. As the domes are of different sizes, it gives the impression of a group of polychromatic puff-balls at various stages of development. After walking round it in stunned silence for half an hour, I came to the conclusion that if Walt Disney had said to a Californian architect 'design me a real Russian cathedral for Disneyland', this is what he would have received. Compared with the tall, elegant, quietly dressed and beautifully coiffured (in gold) inner Kremlin churches, St Basil's is garish, almost vulgar, but with enormous personality. It is as though a group of soignée models in Dior gowns were inside the Kremlin wall, having a well-bred cocktail party, while banished outside, to the edge of Red Square, is this dumpy, jovial cockney Pearly King.

In between all the dull routine stuff we had to do in Moscow before we could start our journey round the Soviet Union, we had one treat that stands out in my mind. That was to meet Nick Drosdov, a tall, elegant and most charming man who is Russia's answer to David Attenborough on television, hosting a most popular monthly nature programme. With his great interest and concern for nature and his delightful, puckish sense of humour he was a joy to meet and to work with, and we thoroughly enjoyed appearing on his show. So, when finally we had tied up all the loose ends and were preparing for the first step in our mammoth journey, we were delighted that Nick came down to the railway station to see us off. It was then that we discovered his endearing habit of carrying a Gladstone bag, which sometimes houses his favourite pet snake but usually contains a series of presents. These are not given to you all at once but at intervals so that you are left entranced and breathless like children with a conjurer. On this occasion he started by taking out a box of chocolates for Lee. Passionate kisses having been exchanged, we chatted about this and that for a while and then Nick dived into his Gladstone bag and produced a box containing six little green glasses each set in a delicate filigree holder in which was embodied a different animal motif. After we had unpacked them and expressed our joy at this charming gift we chatted on for five minutes or so until Nick dived once more into his treasure chest and triumphantly produced a bottle of brandy with which to fill the glasses. I regret to say that we consumed so much of it that Nick almost failed to get off the train as it started and we only just got him out onto the platform in time. It was an auspicious start to our travels.

Overleaf: *A map of the Soviet Union showing the areas we visited.*

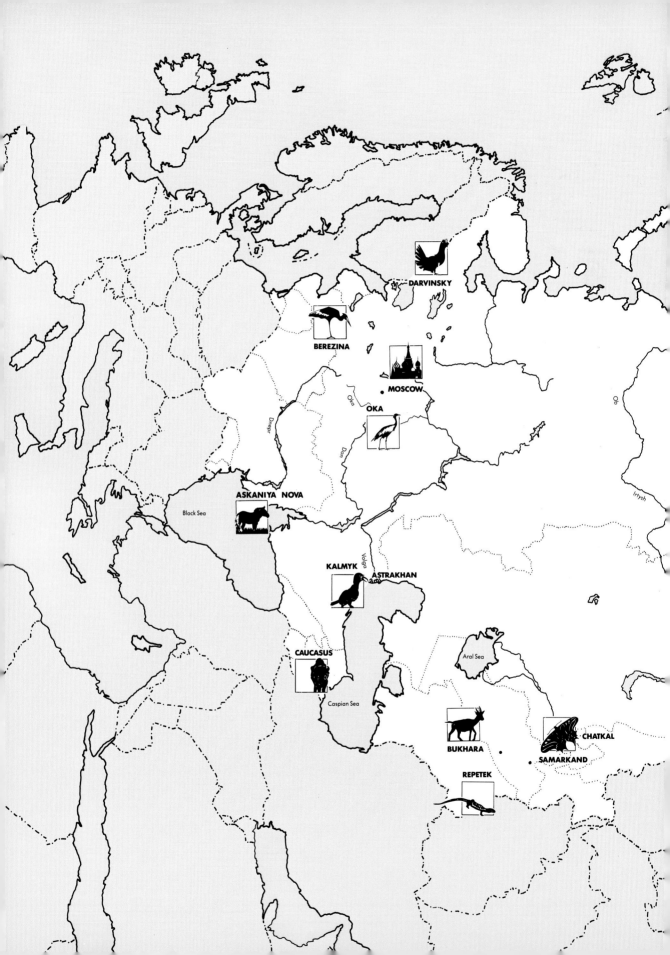

DARVINSKY

BEREZINA

MOSCOW

OKA

Oka

Don

Ob

Irtysh

Dnepr

ASKANIYA NOVA

Black Sea

Volga

KALMYK

ASTRAKHAN

Aral Sea

CAUCASUS

Caspian Sea

BUKHARA

CHATKAL

SAMARKAND

REPETEK

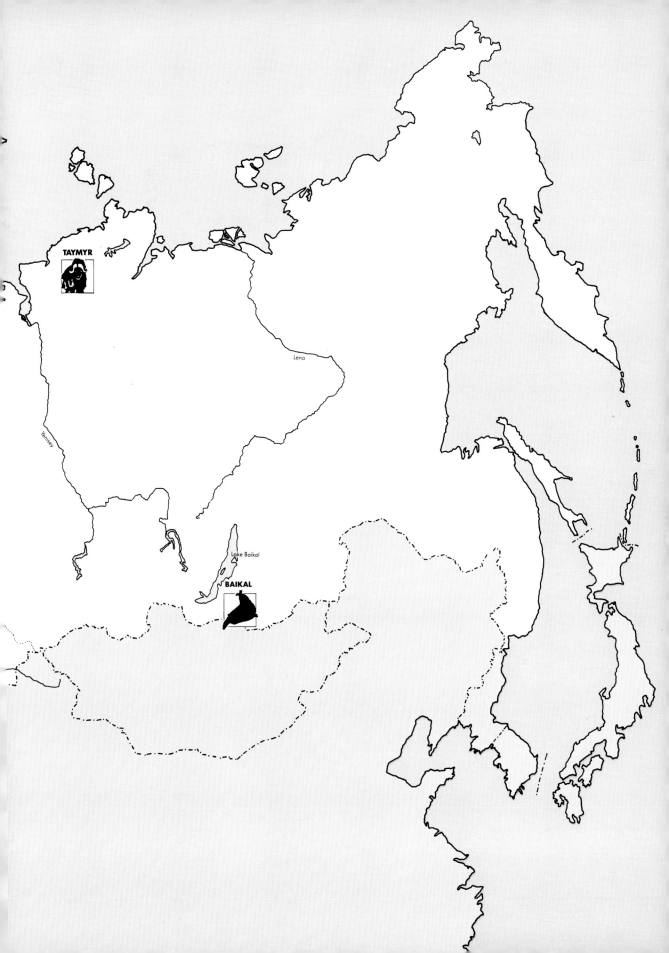

TAYMYR

Yenisey

Lena

Lake Baikal

BAIKAL

DARVINSKY
Song of the capercaillie

ДАРВИНСКИЙ ЗАПОВЕДНИК

DARVINSKY

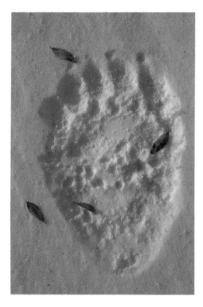

This was all we saw of the elusive Russian bear. Though our splendid cameraman did finally find and film one, we regret to say the only bear we saw in Russia was a tame dancing one in a market.

Preceding page: *The breeding ground for the capercaillie. The breeding programme for the capercaillie* (inset) *has been so successful at Darvinsky that a great number of birds have been returned to the wild.*

THERE were two reasons for us going to the Darvinsky Reserve. Firstly, the reserve had been created to study and monitor the effects on the environment of what is one of the largest man-made lakes in the world, the Rybinsk Reservoir. The second, and slightly more exciting, reason was that the reserve staff had pinpointed a hibernating bear, which they assured us we could film. However, just before we set off – too late to cancel all our plans – we got a depressing telegram informing us that, with a total lack of consideration for our wishes, the bear had woken up and gone walkabout. As we knew the reserve staff (their *amour propre* wounded by this uncooperative symbol of Mother Russia) would be searching frantically for an un-insomniac bear, we decided to go anyway.

We took the night train from Moscow and the next morning arrived in the town of Cherepovets, where the ancient station buildings were pure Regency in design and could have been created by Nash. They were painted a pale sage-green with cream-coloured facings and looked at once elegant and out of place. Behind them reared the rest of the town, a series of huge, grey monolithic apartment buildings, most of which looked half-finished. We were met on the snowy platform by Vasily Nesterenko, the Director of the Reserve, who, with his high-cheekboned Mongolian face and fur hat, looked as though he had come straight from Tibet. Outside the station, there awaited us a lorry, eight jeeps and a police car. We and our equipment were loaded into these vehicles and our entourage set off, led by the police car, blue light flashing, siren blaring, forcing all other traffic into the side of the road and zooming through red traffic lights with gay abandon. Our police escort accompanied us through the town and along the road for some miles beyond. Then, when we had to turn off onto a dirt road, muddy as a ploughed field and encrusted with ice, they chickened out and left us. The road rapidly became a nightmare. Although snow ploughs had been at work, pushing great slabs of snow into piles on each side of the road (like the broken columns of some ancient Greek city), these, and the banks below them, had frozen solid. Thus fresh snow and rain had filled in what was in effect a frozen river-bed from which the water could not escape, so one minute we were driving axle-deep in coffee-coloured water and the next minute through what looked like a badly-made chocolate mousse. Eventually, we turned off this mousse highway onto a smaller, more glutinous one, which led to a tiny village of wooden houses, all one-storey, with wonderful shutters and window frames delightfully carved and painted in gay colours – blue, white, pink and green. They glowed like jewels against the dark wood of the walls and lit up the bleak mud and snow landscape. In one of them we were greeted by a charming old couple in their late seventies, who had prepared lunch for us. He had a face like a walnut

and she had eyes as blue as hedge-sparrow's eggs in a face like brown parchment. We were ushered into their delightful small house – piping hot, since all the big wood-burning stoves built into the walls between the rooms were blazing. On the long table in the main room there had been assembled enough food to succour the Red Army. Cheesecake, buns and blueberry pie, potatoes, meat balls, masses of pickles, chopped-egg sandwiches, rice and egg filled pies, and to drink, a huge samovar for manufacturing tea, cranberry juice and the inevitable vodka without which no meal (including breakfast) would be complete in the Soviet Union. After this delicious repast, we set out again over progressively bad roads through spruce forests so thick that they seemed almost solid, rank after rank of trees, straight as rocket sticks, creating a deeply shadowed, gloomy landscape. However, on the outskirts of the forest were baby spruce two or three feet high, green as billiard tables, their feet buried in snow, their little furry arms outstretched in welcome.

We reached the beginning of the reserve and drove along the edge of the enormous lake, still frozen, that stretched away as far as the eye could see, like pink-tinged cream in the late afternoon sun, with glimmering patches like fish scales where the snow had melted and a tattered fringe of forest at its rim. Finally, we arrived at the large wooden building in which the crew were to live and in which all of us ate. A group of scientists and workers and their wives assembled to give us the traditional greeting and as Lee and I crawled stiffly out of our jeep, a handsome woman came forward bearing a large round flat

The road to Darvinsky was something of a nightmare even though snow ploughs had been at work.

Above: *The traditional greeting of bread and salt. I did not realize that you were supposed to keep the beautifully embroidered napkin on which it is presented and so I left it carefully folded in the kitchen.*

loaf of homemade brown bread and a pot of salt, carefully balanced on a beautifully embroidered red napkin. As no one had prepared me for this, I was uncertain what to do. Fortunately, John arrived in the nick of time and explained that I had to break off two pieces of the bread, dip them in the salt, and then give one piece to Lee and eat the other myself. This I did, amid much laughter, for I almost dropped the bread into the snow, and then Lee and I were led to our own tiny establishment, a log cabin that consisted of a living room, a bedroom and a tiny hallway. We felt rather like newlyweds being escorted to our honeymoon cottage. Once we had settled in and the sky had turned from pink to yellow to velvety black, we made our way over to the main house, scrunching and slipping in the snow and ice, and had a sustaining meal of meat, potatoes, freshly baked brown bread, sweet fresh milk, tea and vodka. Then, replete, we returned to our cottage under a full moon that was making the broken ice glitter and the snow on the lake look as smooth as milk. A solitary dog was barking and the sound echoed over the moonlit lake forlornly.

While waiting for another bear to be discovered, we concentrated on the capercaillie. The size of a small turkey, this splendid bird of the grouse family is kept and bred at Darvinsky to reinforce the wild stocks, which, through overhunting, had diminished drastically. The birds are kept in a series of large aviaries, one massive, aggressive cock bird to three or four hens. We went into the first aviary where the hen birds, feathers coloured like autumn leaves, but with lovely, shining chestnut breasts, crouched and shuffled humbly in the background, while the cock bird, overexcited by our presence, strutted and

Top: *The exquisite carved shutters on the wooden houses were most lovely to look at and in many cases painted gay colours that contrasted beautifully with the dark woodwork of the house.*

The marvellous arrogant display of this wonderful bird is so full of fire and passion that it would, I believe, keep even a hungry wolf at bay.

displayed round us with an arrogance that could only be equalled by a Prussian officer in a new uniform. The uniform in this case was really splendid and so the arrogance was excusable. He was bottle-green on the upper breast, merging into deep shining blue on the neck and head. On the brownish wings were handsome military epaulettes of white. His tail was of deep blue feathers patched with white and this he spread like a crisp Victorian fan at a ball. He ran around us on his heavy, flat feet, his legs encased in pantaloons of feathers, his head thrown back, showing the caramel-coloured hawk-like beak and his fierce, bristling beard of black feathers. His wild hazel-coloured eyes were surmounted by the most startling eyebrows, fleshy, carunculated scarlet patches of skin like new moons that gave him a most military appearance. As he ran and paused, ran and paused around us, he produced two completely different sounds. It was almost as if he were a ventriloquist, using one voice for the question and another voice for the answer. The first sound was a deep, tonking noise, like someone carefully dropping chestnuts onto a drum. After a slight pause, this was answered by the extraordinary nasal bubble, reminiscent of the sinus-inflicted cries of Punch in the old-fashioned Punch and Judy shows. With head thrown back, feathery beard on end, fierce beak open, red eyebrows raised in wrath at our intrusion, it was an extraordinarily heraldic sight – the sort of bird a medieval knight would have emblazoned on his shield. So, having spent a couple of hours with these magnificent creatures, we returned to our cottage, heartened by the news that another bear had been found, but distressed that we would have to get up at three a.m. to start off in pursuit of it at four.

We dragged ourselves out of bed to find it was snowing, although the temperature had risen in the night. Five skidoos (rather like a motorbike with tank tracks on it, noisy, smelly, but fast) had been assembled. One of them dragged a flat sledge with some of the equipment while another pulled a sledge that looked like a cross

I think it was the braveness of the bird that impressed us most. Here is the cock bird doing his operatic act almost in our laps. You felt he would not have hesitated to peck you to death if he caught you casting covetous eyes on one of his hens.

You can see from the beauty of this hen bird why the cock capercaillie gets into such a frenzy firstly to attract them and secondly to keep them once he has them. Though not as flamboyant as the cock bird's plumage, it is a beautiful and subtle arrangement of colours, and it shows up against the snow like a delicate pile of autumn leaves.

between a giant infant's crib and the sort of sleigh Father Christmas is wont to use. The back of this monster construction had been filled with hay and lambskin rugs and into it Lee and I were installed (like Tsar and Tsarina), together with the more delicate equipment. We set off through the fine, driving snow and in the pale yellow and purple dawn light the lake looked immense, with the rim of forest crouched black and malevolent-looking on the further shore. After a couple of hours' travel, it became patently obvious that we were not going to be able to keep our rendezvous with the bear. Rising temperature had softened the layer of snow so that, instead of gliding over it, both skidoos and sledges were constantly breaking through the crust of snow and sticking. However, a mile or two further on, we were assured, there was a remote forester's house where we could have some breakfast and review the situation.

It was at this point that the raccoon dog entered our lives. Vasily, who had got increasingly depressed at the non-cooperation of bears and the disinclination of the weather to obey him, suddenly, like a conjurer, whipped open the boot of his skidoo and produced from it a half-grown raccoon dog, which he dumped into my lap with a flourish. It crouched there with the same expression of shock on its face that I must have been wearing, for the last raccoon dog I had been on intimate terms with was one that I looked after when I was a student keeper at Whipsnade, some forty years ago. These attractive creatures are extremely interesting canines and their introduction and consequent spread throughout Europe is a perfect example of man's stupidity and unnecessary tinkering with nature. These animals, with

It was an austere but beautiful landscape made as immobile as an etching by ice and snow.

As the thaw was setting in, the weight of our Father Christmas sleigh kept breaking through the snow crust and had to be hauled out by hand.

their short legs, look like very hairy corgis with a raccoon-like face. They were once confined to Japan and eastern Asia and then somebody had the bright idea that if they were introduced into the forest areas of western Russia they would be a valuable fur-bearing creature. So they were introduced and, being an omnivore with a penchant for survival, soon spread over the whole of middle Europe and became a pest. To add insult to injury, it was then discovered that their skin was useless, so Europe had acquired a large pest to the detriment of its natural fauna, in the same way that it had acquired the South American coypu or nutria. Man is forever meddling with nature in a stupid fashion.

The raccoon dog lay in my lap and allowed me to stroke it, appearing to be perfectly content, but then Vasily appeared with a large dog collar and leash and attempted to put them on the animal. The raccoon dog decided that this was too much of an indignity. With a quick wriggle and a jump, it rocketed out of my lap and over the side of the sledge. Once on the ice, its furry feet gave it terrific purchase and it set off across the lake at a smart, determined trot that soon had it about a hundred yards away. Everyone set off in pursuit, but they were not nearly as agile as the raccoon dog and soon the ice was littered with fallen bodies. In the end they had to return to the skidoos and, mounting them, used them to surround and recapture our raccoon dog. He was bundled back into the boot to be filmed on the following day, for the sky was now so overcast and the snowfall so heavy that it precluded all thoughts of filming. I noticed a curious thing: the snowflakes that were falling (each one about three times the size of a pinhead) were shaped like tiny flowers with five petals, each petal filigreed in the most minute and intricate fashion so that the flowers looked as though they were made out of lace. Very soon, the dark

Crouched in our laps is the raccoon dog, which seconds later took off across the ice and caused us so much trouble to recapture – and it had the bad grace to escape the following morning.

sheepskin rug over our laps was covered in these tiny snowflakes so it looked like a field of miniature daisies.

We eventually reached the forester's house, where we had a most welcome meal and drank gallons of sustaining tea. After this, we decided to return home, for the weather was getting worse and worse and so our chances of filming a bear, even if we saw one, were nil. We had progressed a few miles on our homeward journey when the skidoo that was pulling us rounded a snow bank at too acute an angle, whereupon our massive Father Christmas sledge turned turtle, precipitating me, Lee and all our delicate equipment out onto the ice in a welter of sheepskin rugs and hay. Fortunately, neither we nor our equipment were hurt, but the poor forester who was driving us was chagrined and ashamed of himself, and it took a lot of hugging and kissing to persuade him not to commit suicide out of mortification.

The following day was a disaster. The raccoon dog had escaped and the crew tried to film wild capercaillie with no success. Then in the afternoon I had promised to give a talk to the assembled foresters and their families about our work. As this is a reserve called after Charles Darwin, there was naturally a large, heavily framed portrait of that distinguished scientist hanging on the wall opposite me in the room where I gave my talk. I had just been asked if I thought there should be more captive breeding centres in the world like the one I had set up in Jersey and I was launching enthusiastically into my reply, when the massive portrait fell off the wall with a crash that shook the building and filled everybody with alarm and consternation.

Darvinsky, though a fascinating place, was not one of our more successful shoots.

OKA
Flood rescue

OKA

OKA

The crane family, including some of the largest and most beautiful birds in the world, are nearly all declining in numbers, partly because all along the complex and extensive migration routes that they have followed from time immemorial they are harried and killed, and partly because so many of their feeding and breeding grounds – the rich swamplands and grasslands – are being drained, falling under the plough and being doused with insecticides. Seven of the fourteen species of the world's cranes nest in the Soviet Union, including all those pictured here.

Preceding page: Oka still frost-bound, and later, the river in flood (inset).

THE reserve at Oka lies some three hundred miles from Moscow and we reached it by train and bus. Travelling like this gives you some impression of the vastness of Russia, which you can never obtain by flying, and you can also see so much more. The landscape was flat, thickly wooded in most places, snow-covered and bleak. In the towns we passed through, the tiny weatherboard houses were charming. They looked as though each one had been designed and built for a dwarf. They were colourful and blended into the landscape, unlike the great, grey or brown, unfinished-looking high-rise apartment blocks that loomed over them. We passed by a huge marshland where the ice and snow were thawing out and breaking up, the pieces like a great, white jigsaw, moving slowly under an iron-grey sky, flecked with huge flocks of starlings.

We arrived at Ryazan in the late afternoon and drove the rest of the way in a huge bus. We passed through a number of villages, streets deeply rutted, awash with the melting ice, the little wooden houses crouching in the snow like abandoned apiaries, with here and there the occasional light showing, like a glow-worm. The sky was tangerine-coloured in the setting sun and across it flew flocks of rooks mournfully lamenting the dying day. We arrived late, but found the most comfortable accommodation awaiting us, and a delicious meal.

The following morning we went to see one of the things Oka is famous for – its crane collection. Here, in spacious paddocks, were housed white-naped, demoiselle, hooded and the extremely rare Siberian cranes. These latter were procured from Siberia as eggs, hatched at Oka and then hand-reared. They are magnificent birds, nearly five feet high, very proud and aggressive. When we went into the pen with them the male threw his head back, beak clattering, his body trembling, his wings and tail stretched out, crisp as a crinoline. He gave wild, harsh cries like Maria Callas being stabbed with a penknife and the other Siberians answered him, so the paddock echoed with their song. His display over, he started his slow, ritual pacing, the sort of thing you see soldiers doing when following a funeral cortege. Next, we visited the hooded cranes, who were only half-grown and very tame. They walked round and round us very delicately, making purring noises that sounded more like cats than birds, and gently pecked food from our hands.

Once we had visited the cranes, filmed them and been sung to by them, we went to see the bird of prey collection, which is the largest in Russia and which, as well as having various falcons and golden eagles, had several pairs of one of the most beautiful birds of prey in the world, the lammergeier, or bearded vulture. They are enormous and have a sort of fierce majesty about them that makes them quite one of the most impressive birds I have ever seen. Their black beards and fiery-red

rim of the eye give them a piratical look, yet the colouring on their wings was like a delicate waterfall of pale brown feathers. The name lammergeier means sheep-stealer, and in Spain this bird is called by the rather tongue-twisting name of quebrantahuesos, meaning 'bonecracker', because of its habit of carrying large bones and skulls up to a height and dropping them onto rocks below in order to split them so it can extract the marrow and brains with its peculiarly shaped tongue. In many parts of Greece tortoises are its chief prey and these are treated in the same way as bones or skulls.

Next door to the lammergeiers lived a pair of griffon vultures. The cockbird was immense and ridiculously tame, and the moment you entered the aviary he would rush forward in a sort of lop-sided hobble to greet you. With this arthritic movement, combined with his uncombed-looking feathers, his large domed head covered with fine brown down and his scrawny bluish-grey neck, he looked like one of those elderly erudite scholars that you see inhabiting the Athenaeum Club. He was an absurd and enchanting bird: scratch his massive head and beak and he would go into a trance, his yellowish eyes would glaze and his wings would start to tremble in ecstasy; start to tickle his ribs under his wings and he would get hysterical, uttering loud wheezes, gasps and prolonged giggles such as a child makes when you tickle it, and would fall at your feet, prostrate with mirth, begging you to desist and yet at the same time longing for you to go on. He was quite one of the most enchanting and amusing of birds. We spent half an hour filming him and he behaved like a born star. He fell on the floor and giggled, he went into a trance when you scratched him, he paced to and fro on the ground, hunch-backed in his gown of feathers like some octogenarian professor. He flew up onto his perch and paced along it carefully, giving the impression that he was going to fall off in a flurry of feathers at any moment. Having done his bit for the camera, he then

Above left: *Hooded crane*

Top: *White-naped crane*

Above: *Demoiselle crane*

Above: *The Siberian crane did his wonderful display for us, head back, beak open, wings dropped and rustling like bales of silk being unrolled.*

Above right: *These graceful, delicate young hooded cranes did not seem to feel the cold at all, while we were muffled up to the eyebrows in warm clothing.*

Opposite: *The griffon vulture (top), who giggled when tickled, is doing his tightrope act for us here. The wonderful corsair's profile of the lammergeier, or 'bone-cracker', (bottom right) one of the most handsome birds of prey in the world. Among the birds of prey here, the smallest but one of the smartest was the dapper peregrine falcon (bottom left).*

confessed that his wife (who had been watching his antics with an air of disdain) did not really understand him and he felt that Lee – though not possessing feathers – was really more to his taste. So, seizing the hem of her coat, he endeavoured to drag her further into the aviary with heaven knows what evil avian thoughts in mind. Fortunately, with a quick tickle I managed to distract him and so this avicultural elopement never came to fruition.

One of the many extraordinary activities of Oka, and one which we had come especially to film, was their great annual rescue operation. As winter ends and the iron-like grip of the ice and snow softens, the Oka River swells with this additional burden of moisture and bursts its banks, flooding out over the flatlands like molten glass, catching and trapping on minute islands and on grassy knolls animals who – though they are capable of swimming – in their weakened winter state cannot swim the enormous distances that would take them to safety, dry land and a good food supply. Thus you get a host of mammalian refugees dotted about, shipwrecked as it were, like so many Robinson Crusoes, who have to be rescued before they perish. So as the ice cracks and melts and the sherry-coloured waters creep up around the trees, the flotilla of boats at Oka is put into operation.

As usual when you are trying to film, something seems to go against you. In this instance, when the floods should have been in full spate there was a sudden cold snap that refroze parts of the melting ice and trapped all the boats at their moorings. However, the director was not faint-hearted and was determined that we should accomplish what we had come for, so he mustered all the available foresters and simply had the boats lifted out of the ice and dragged through a couple of miles of forest to a place where the river was in flood and they could be launched. When launched, the boats were quite far from the bank and this left a stretch of water, mud and ice that had to be crossed before we could get to them. The director was terribly shocked at my intention of wading out, so, resourceful as ever, he detailed one of the foresters to carry Lee and myself. The man he chose was a young giant, standing some 6 feet 7 inches, and as muscular as a dinosaur. He had a

The thaw begins (above) and so does the work of rescuing the 'Robinson Crusoe' animals on the islands created by the immense floods. Opposite: We moved in the boats over flooded meadows, still with patches of ice on them, the trees standing knee-deep in water like people on holiday paddling in the sea. The muffs of the pussywillows were bursting into flower (inset left), the first sign of spring, and the muskrats (inset right) were perfectly happy since they could all swim well and dive to the drowned meadows for food.

Preceding page: That night the river froze when we least expected it, locking our boats in ice, so they had to be cut free and dragged through the forest to an ice-free stretch of water. (inset) I was carried piggyback to our boat by our gentle giant, who later gave me the coat he was wearing.

handsome, smiling face and was wearing an extraordinarily nice sheepskin coat. Ignoring my protestations, he simply picked me up as if I weighed no more than a bundle of feathers, carried me out, dumped me in the boat and then waded back and performed the same service for Lee. Having been chosen as our giant for the day made him very proud and so he stayed close to us, ready to pluck us up in his arms should there be the slightest danger to our royal persons. At a later stage in the proceedings I was admiring his coat and so he solemnly took it off and gave it to me and no argument on my part would make him take it back. I found out later that these coats are custom built and cost about £250. It cured me of admiring anything else the whole time I was in Russia.

So our six-strong armada set off down the river through the drowned landscape, trees up to their armpits in brown water, huge rafts of ice and snow up in the hedges, each unpleasantly grey and forlorn-looking like bits of Miss Haversham's wedding cake. Sun glittered and flecked the water, the engines purred and there was the occasional hissing scrunch as we hit a miniature field of melting ice and mud, which was like ploughing your way through a bowl of brown sugar. Mats of branches and dead winter vegetation were pushed like forlorn wigs into crevices amid the trees and bushes, and on many of these sat brown rotund muskrats feeding eagerly on green grass, which they were obtaining by diving down to the drowned meadows beneath the flood waters. Everything seemed to be excited by the sun and the breakup of winter's cold stranglehold on the land. Pussy-willow flowers, which up to now had resembled sedate miniature Edwardian

Unlike the muskrats, creatures like badgers (below), foxes (bottom) and raccoon dogs (right) could not swim well, and so needed the help of our 'ambulance' service.

ladies' muffs, were turning into tiny gardens of butter-yellow blooms. Skylarks, as exuberant as children released from school, were building ladders of song in the sky and then, Icarus-like, falling into the green meadows so newly emerged from their snow shroud. Wagtails in small flocks danced across the floating ice like a delicate twinkling ballet and in the upper trees the rooks chanted solemnly.

After we had travelled for an hour or so, we reached an area where the flood was immense, stretching away as far as the eye could see, dotted with tiny islands and the top halves of the trees. This was where our rescue operations began. On one tiny island we found an exhausted raccoon dog, and he made little attempt to escape. He was soon caught in a sort of gigantic butterfly net and then transferred to a wire cage. A few islands further on we discovered a marooned badger and set about the task of rounding him up. He was extremely morose and in no way was he going to take kindly to our rescue attempts. He waddled about sniffing and groaning and, when finally cornered, showed his gratitude by biting the hand of one of the foresters quite badly before being manoeuvred into a sack. Our next reluctant castaway was a fox with a rich red winter coat and savagely snarling muzzle. He, like the badger, fought off our attempts at rescue, growling in a deep voice and biting at everything that came within range, his white teeth snapping together like castanets. We transported our three creatures to the edge of the flood area and let them go. The raccoon dog lay in a quivering heap, obviously thinking his last hour had come, and we actually had to shoo him away. In contrast, the badger came out of his sack like a fur-covered bulldozer and trundled away across the meadows without a backward glance, sniffing and snorting disdainfully to himself. The fox emerged from his sack with a certain amount of caution and when he saw that he had the chance of freedom, he galloped off, his tail like a flame against the green of the grass. He reached a slight rise in the ground and got behind it, where he stopped for ten minutes or so,

looking back at us, only the top of his head and his ears showing.

It was at this point, while we were squatting in the sunshine, eating our sandwiches and trying to keep the cold and damp out with the inevitable vodka, that our indefatigable director suddenly produced a surprise for me, and what a wonderful surprise it was. It was a creature I had long wanted to meet – a Russian desman. These extraordinary insectivores are about the size of a large guinea pig, clad in dark, soft, mole-like fur. Being aquatic, they have strong, fully webbed feet with large claws and a heavy, hairless tail, flattened from side to side like a tadpole's. Probably the most astonishing thing about the desman is its head, and particularly its nose. The ears are small, embedded in the thick fur, and the eyes are rudimentary, merely black dots on the pale skin, like a pair of black pinheads, but the nose is superb, long and resembling a hairy elephant's trunk, trumpet-shaped and astonishingly mobile, sweeping from side to side like a Geiger counter, standing up on end or else curving itself into a Fagin-like sickle. He was, like all insectivores, hyperactive, his body throbbing like a newly caught bird, his feet scrabbling on my coat, his whiffling nose exploring every nook and cranny of my clothing in the hopes of finding something edible. These charming creatures were once almost exterminated for the sake of their beautiful pelts but fortunately, in the nick of time, the danger was recognized by the Soviet authorities and a ban on their capture was introduced. Today the numbers of desman are increasing.

We released him in a large, very shallow pond so we could film him underwater, and he behaved beautifully. As he slid into the water his fur became sleek and silvery with bubbles, his powerful tail wagged from side to side, just as a tadpole's does. He scrabbled in the muddy bottom with his webbed feet, hoping to dislodge snails or similar prey and he whiffled his ridiculous nose to and fro with all the enthusiasm of a newly-wed housewife with her first vacuum cleaner. Of all the many entrancing animals we met in Russia, I think the desman is the one species I would have liked to have brought home to Jersey.

As the afternoon wore on we rescued more and more animals – hares, rabbits, hedgehogs and similar beasts. Then, as the setting sun flooded the sky with daffodil-yellow light, we chugged homeward across the dark flood waters chequered with rafts of floating ice.

The one enchanting and ridiculous-looking creature in Russia we would have liked to have brought home with us – the Russian desman, the captivating E.T. of the insectivores.

BEREZINA
Children in nature

БЕРЕЗИНА
BEREZINA

The Berezina reserve is famous for its beavers, its black storks and its flowers (above and opposite). It was originally set up to protect the beavers when it was discovered that their populations were declining all over the Soviet Union because of overhunting. So successful was the programme that beavers from Berezina were once used to re-stock other Soviet reserves. The outlook for the black stork, however, is not so optimistic.

Preceding page: The Berezina River and (inset) in the forest for a botany lesson with local schoolchildren.

WE wanted to see and film a Russian river in the full flush of summer, and so in late June we headed west into White Russia and the Berezina Reserve. To get there we had to fly to Minsk (which, like so many Russian towns, is impossible to write a limerick about) and then take a two-hour drive through lovely undulating country of mixed woodland and fields, the hedgerow lined with ranks of wild lupins of a pale bluey-mauve shade that was quite lovely against the dark trees.

The reserve, situated on the Berezina River, was established in 1925 in order to preserve the beaver, an animal that, due principally to over-hunting, was in dire straits and might well have become extinct if protection had not come in time. Now there are over six hundred living permanently on the reserve and so prolific are they that in the 1950s and 1960s over a thousand specimens were sent to stock reserves all over Russia. We also wanted to see and film the beautiful black stork, a rare and secretive bird that nested here.

After we had settled into the headquarters, they piled us into boats so that we could go and investigate the river. The beginning of our journey, however, was down a beautiful, reedy, waterlily-choked canal, a-glitter with dragonflies. This canal, constructed in the days of Catherine the Great, was one of a series designed in a grandoise plan to knit the various river and lake systems together so that the Baltic could be linked up with the Black Sea. It was fascinating to think, as we drifted down its weedy, bird-haunted length, that at one time steamers and barges had slowly traversed its clear water, coming from one end of Russia to the other, bringing rich cargoes in their holds and carrying an extraordinary array of passengers. What a wonderful trip it must have been, to travel gently and sedately through the heart of this vast country.

Eventually, to my disappointment, the canal ended, but then we were out in the Berezina River itself, wearing a handsome scarf of reeds and its banks dotted here and there with huge, ancient willows, which, as they turned over their leaves in the breeze, changed from green to silver and back again. We saw many beaver lodges, huge domes of twigs and branches cemented together with mud, but the occupants remained stubbornly absent. However, one compensation, as we drifted down the lily-studded waters, was to see a black stork fly out from a group of trees and, looking in silhouette strangely like a pterodactyl, flap slowly down the river. We were very excited at this sighting so you can imagine our gloom when, on returning to headquarters, we learnt that the three baby black storks we were to film had been eaten by ravens. My respect and admiration for ravens reached a very low ebb at this news, for not only did it affect our filming, but there were only seven known nests of the stork in the whole reserve, so the loss of these three nestlings was a major tragedy in

every respect. However, the charming young ornithologist assured us that they were out looking for another nest in an accessible place for filming and with this somewhat cold comfort we had to be content.

While waiting for a black stork's nest to be discovered and in between intermittent attempts to film the reluctant beavers, we investigated the local school.

This proved to be enchanting. To begin with, the school was a normal one but heavily orientated towards ecology and conservation. We discovered the children were taught about such things as forestry and environmental protection in a practical manner. Moreover, they

Catherine the Great's canal, now an overgrown backwater, rich in plant and animal life, once throbbed to the sound of steamer engines carrying cargos from one end of Russia to the other. Now only frogs croak and birds call and all is peaceful.

had their own farm with everything from beehives to cows, and this they worked themselves under the guidance of their teachers. On the reserve they had a little zoo with paddocks containing various wild fauna, such as deer, wild boar and some European bison. In 1974 six bison had been introduced into the reserve and, they told us proudly, the herd now numbered twenty-three. It was the children's job to provide fodder for these and other beasts during the severest winters, and they made hay from the lush grasses that grew beneath the apple trees in their orchard. As it had been a very long time since I went haymaking — far too long — we piled a group of these charming bright-eyed kids into an old school bus and went a-haying, as they used to say in Hampshire. Some of the kids spoke a little English but were rather shy of their accomplishment. But with the aid of that indispensable diplomatic tool, chewing gum, we broke down the barriers. As we bumped along, they sang songs about conservation in a charming amalgam of tremulous sopranos and told us about their activities. They also told us, as all children do, stories to curdle our blood and stretch our imagination and credulity to their limits.

Probably the tale of the bear was the best, even though it had a sad and sanguine ending. Their beehives, they explained, were arranged under the apple trees, where we were now going to go a-haying. Early in the winter before last they had come one day to find a beehive had been plundered. It lay disembowelled on the ground, the bees dead with cold, the honey from splintered combs forming pools on the frozen grass. Round it, ominous as thunderclouds, were the great footprints of a bear. They hoped it was a bear that was passing through on its way to its hibernation lair far away, but the weight and authority of the footprints, the way they had cracked the early winter ice, augured not good but evil. By now, of course, the whole bus was filled with menace. My favourite of the girls, a diminutive creature with huge china-blue eyes and a ridiculous Edwardian straw hat with ribbons on it that made

Although we saw plenty of evidence of beavers in the shape of their lodges (left), they themselves remained stubbornly invisible. However, as compensation, we did see a group of black storks (below) flying across the river.

her look irresistible, was visualizing the bear so vividly that her wonderful blue eyes were almost falling out into her lap. So, the story continued, they came the following day and found another beehive crushed and dead, its delicious combs eaten, the bees lying in the frozen air, twitching on their way to death. And on the next day a similar desecration of a hive had happened. It was terrible, for at this rate all their hives would vanish. They had to put a stop to the bear's apiarist activities – it had to be shot. But, I protested, looking at my Edwardian girl, was it not a Russian bear? Was it not a terrible thing to kill a Russian bear? Yes, she agreed, her eyes so wide they looked like the Mediterranean itself, but you had to have beehives and if bears interfered then they must be stopped.

We had now reached the denouement of this tale and everyone was joining in, and what with the sound of the old bus's engine and ten shrill voices trying to tell us what happened, it was some time before we grasped the salient points. Early one morning an ambush party assembled in the apple orchard and as at dawn the bear shouldered its way towards the beehives, walking in the wrestler's slouch that bears adopt, a single bullet ended its life. But triumph was short-lived, for when the carcass was examined it was discovered why this bear had developed such a taste for honey. It was an ancient bear, one so old that it had lost all its teeth and so could no longer kill deer or other game. It was now reduced to eating moss and berries and other soft things until it discovered the bounty of the beehives. If it had been allowed to go on plundering the beehives, this would have only lasted a short time, as then the bleak winter would have overtaken it and it would have died anyway, for it could not have built up a sufficient layer of fat to sustain it during the long hibernation. So perhaps the shooting of it was a mercy. But the thought of a toothless octogenarian bear robbing beehives so that it could suck in the sustaining honey and thus meeting its death was a rather sad image.

Overleaf: We shall remember the whole of the Soviet Union for its wealth of flowers but nowhere was more flower-bedecked than Berezina. Flowers were everywhere so that you feared to walk in case you crushed some brilliant and delicate blossom. Fields of yellow wild lupins stretched as far as the eye could see and were a dazzlingly beautiful sight. Inset: Red helleborine (top left), lesser butterfly orchid (centre left), Ivan and Maria (bottom left), mountain arnica (right), columbine (bottom right).

When we reached the orchards the children described how the hay was gathered. First, when the grass was high enough, the field in which the apple trees stood was scythed by the older children and the teachers. They were busy at work in the corner of the orchard and the sight of scythes being used was a delight, better than any smelly mechanical contrivance. The rhythmic, almost ballet-like movements of the body, the smooth swish of the blade like someone cutting a bale of silk, and the rich, heady aroma of the fallen grasses and herbs were wonderful. Once the grass had been scythed into neat rows, the younger children had to turn it in the sun so that it became toasted and dry and fit for the hay wagon to take it away and turn into blonde haystacks.

After we had finished our aromatic task of turning the hay and picked the burrs and beetles out of our trousers, we took some of the hay up to the children's little zoo to feed the bison and deer, who were delighted with this fresh, juicy fodder. Then, accompanied by the zoo botanist, Lyuba, we went to look for flowers in the forest, and the children scattered in front of us like hounds, searching out wild strawberries for us to eat. As we munched and got strawberry-stained mouths, Lyuba discovered and showed us treasures in the under-growth, plants that were not only rare and beautiful to look at but had fascinating names: Red Helleborine, for example, which was more purple than red, and the Lesser Butterfly Orchid, beautifully white and delicate and no doubt receiving its name from its resemblance to a butterfly although in actual fact it is pollinated by moths. Then there was the Columbine of the buttercup family, a tall, handsome purple flower bearing no resemblance to the canary-yellow buttercups of my youth, and the Mountain Arnica (doubtless a cure-all) looking like a yellow daisy. Consulting our little guide book I was struck (not for the first time) by the imaginative use of names given by botanists when christening plants. We did not meet with the Bulbous Fumewort, the Common Coral Wort, the Herb Frankincense, the Lesser Twayblade or the Common Polypody, but how we wished we had. I must confess, though it was a privilege to see the rare plants and they were all very beautiful, I lost my heart to a common weed, which was not only beautiful but had such a romantic story connected to it. It was called Ivan and Maria, and in the middle of the stalk you had tiny yellow snapdragon-like flowers and above them the leaves started as green and ended up being purple and silver at the tip of the stalk. It looked like two plants in one and according to legend this is exactly what it is. In ancient times Ivan and Maria (from two different villages) fell desperately, irretrievably in love. But alas, for some malevolent tsarist reason, they could not marry. But they asked God to unite them in death as they could not be united in life, and so they returned to earth as the two-fold flower, Maria as the delicate blossoms, Ivan as the sturdy green, purple and silver leaves.

We had a wonderful time with both the flowers and the children, and when we returned to the headquarters we were greeted with the good news that another – and accessible – black stork's nest had been located for us. The next morning we set off early and drove out into the

We went to visit the local school, which is heavily conservation-orientated. The children run their own farm and with them we went hay-making in the sunny apple orchards.

forest. Generally, these birds, being so secretive, tend to nest in the most inaccessible places, but this nest was, strangely enough, only about a quarter of a mile from the road. Here the floor of the forest was covered with a thick eiderdown of moss in bright green and gold and on this grew a miniature forest of blueberries, just coming into fruit, and so we ate as we walked. Here again, there were wild flowers in profusion, ones like drifts of lace, some like minute yellow and white foxgloves, tiny vivid blue ones and others that looked like Victorian velvet pincushions in various shades of purple and wine-red. Presently we came to a clearing in the forest. On one side of it grew an enormous ash tree and in amongst its branches, some forty feet up, was the stork's nest.

It was an enormous structure some four feet deep and about six feet across. It was obviously an old nest that had been lovingly added to over the years as each new breeding season came around. We moved cautiously round the tree until we could get a good view and we could see, squatting in the nest, two fat baby storks. They were still in their dirty whitish baby plumage and had long yellow beaks. They peered down at us solemnly and forlornly, as if they had all the cares of the world on their hunched shoulders. They obviously viewed us with some suspicion, for as we moved round the tree so they revolved in the nest. After we had watched them for some time, we left Rodney there to see if he could get shots of the parent birds, and we made our way over the brilliant mossy carpet to the road, eating handfuls of blueberries as we went.

ASKANIYA NOVA
Last of the virgin steppe

АСКАНИЯ-НОВА
ASKANIYA NOVA

How wonderful this part of the country must have been to the early settlers, a carpet of flowers stretching as far as the eye could see, fragrant and colourful.

'DEAR reader! No matter whether you are an inhabitant of Arkangelsk or Grodno, Riga or Yalta, Paris or Washington, you were and are surrounded by nature, either "wild" or cultured, so dear to everybody that it may make one cry, nature which is unique to everybody, remembered during wanderings in far away countries, together with singular reminiscences of childhood, with the first love and happiness. '

So charmingly starts the English guide book to one of the best-known of the Soviet reserves, Askaniya Nova.

This reserve is situated on the steppes of the Ukraine and, as a matter of fact, preserves in most of its 27,500 acres one of the last areas of pure untouched steppe left in the world. The history of Askaniya Nova is quite remarkable. Catherine the Great, that extraordinary monarch, was trying to get settlers into the vast empty areas of steppe that spread around the Black Sea, and a young penniless German, Johann Fein, took up her offer. To try to establish a farm in such a remote district with such bleak and savage winters was a brave endeavour but one that, nevertheless, succeeded. So prosperous did the Fein family become that the son of Johann bought a nearby sheep farm called Askaniya Nova. His great-great-grandson began the work that Askaniya Nova is now famous for. Animals that had become rare in Russia were brought here to try to build up their numbers by careful breeding. Exotic animals were imported from all over the world, the object being not only to see whether they would acclimatize successfully but whether, by cross-breeding, they could help improve domestic stock and whether (as in the case of the East African eland) they could be domesticated themselves and prove a useful addition to farming around the world. Askaniya Nova was so successful that Tsar Nicholas II paid it a visit, during which he was pecked by a great bustard. In spite of that he raised the Fein family to the aristocracy, a rather unfortunate gesture, because it meant that after the Revolution they had to leave Russia. However, everyone realized the importance of the work being done, and so Askaniya Nova was taken over and continued to expand and prosper.

We had a good flight to Odessa but unfortunately missed our boat for the next stage of the journey, so we had to wait for the hydrofoil. I did not mind, however, for it gave me a chance to admire the huge steps leading down to the dockside on which the famous 'Odessa steps sequence' had been filmed in that epic of Russian cinema, *Battleship Potemkin*. The hydrofoil was swift and extremely comfortable. At the other end we were decanted into a bus and, in the twilight, we travelled over vast steppes carved up into gigantic fields, each one (I was glad to see) guarded by carefully planted windbreaks of trees.

I had long wanted to visit Askaniya Nova, for I had heard and read

Preceding page: The last piece of virgin steppe left in the world, and (inset) one of its inhabitants, Przewalski's horse

about it for many years. I am not quite sure what I expected but I was certainly much surprised to find a flourishing township with a huge administration building, blocks of flats for the scientists and other workers, wide streets laid out with beautiful rose beds planted down them, and blocks of laboratories and research units.

The following morning we were taken on a conducted tour so that we could decide what aspect of the activities we wanted to film. We first of all went to the zoo. Askaniya Nova is really a zoo within a zoo within a farm and it requires a certain mental agility to adjust to this situation at first, since things tend to get slightly muddled, for one minute you are looking at a pure-bred zebra and the next minute at something that looks like the extinct quagga of crossword-puzzle fame but is in reality a cross between a zebra and a horse.

The zoo we visited was a conventional one with cages, paddocks and aviaries, ponds and lakes laid out as they would be in any comparatively small town zoo, but they had some magnificent specimens. The breeding groups of demoiselle cranes were elegant and decorative, as were their chicks. There were some wonderful, imperious-looking whooper swans which, whenever we got too close to the wire, lived up to their name in a loud and military fashion, warning us away from their flocks of young, who looked as though they had been constructed out of yellow dandelion heads. But the most beautiful of all the birds we saw were the great bustards.

We were privileged to go into the paddock and meet seven of them, magnificent birds the size of a turkey, who clustered round us to take bread from our hands. Their bellies were whitish, fading to pale

Exotic animals were first brought to Askaniya Nova in the 1880s to find out whether they could acclimatize to steppe conditions. Many species succeeded, like the Indian nilgai, South American llamas, African eland and Przewalski's horse from Mongolia.

The small zoo at Askaniya Nova keeps many species. The imperious whooper swan, largest of the swans, is so graceful-looking on the water, but on land it looks like a debutante in Wellington boots. Their numbers are decreasing and now there is a total ban on hunting them.

Among the exotic birds kept at Askaniya Nova is this most colourful pheasant (above). The bar-headed goose (right) is a rare species in the Soviet Union.

slate-grey on the throat, neck and head. In the males the long moustaches of feathers that grew from their cheeks and projected beyond the back of the head were also greyish. But it was on the back, wings and tail that the colours were so pure and exquisite. The basic ground colour varied from bronze to beige and imprinted on it were wave-like markings in dark grey and black, flecked here and there with white. The effect was that of a black sea edging its way in tiny wavelets over a smooth sandy shore. Any painter who could capture – with any degree of accuracy – the bird's plumage on canvas would make a fortune. I have seen many birds, from birds-of-paradise to sparrows, that have intricate and lovely plumage, but for elegance and taste I have never seen anything to equal the great bustard. In a paddock full of birds it would have been as obvious as the only woman at a cocktail party who was wearing a Louis Feraud gown. They are trying to reintroduce this marvellous bird into areas of the steppes where it has been exterminated, either by overhunting or by the spread of agriculture. Five of these birds had been hatched from eggs found in nests in areas that were due to fall under the plough and so had been sought out and brought to the centre to form the nucleus of their captive breeding group. The other two had been found during the previous very severe winter, frozen and starving, and had been brought back to the centre to be nursed back to health and strength, with what success we witnessed when their keeper endeavoured to chivvy the cock bird into a more suitable position for photography with the aid of a sack. The cock bird treated the sack as if it were another male bustard

Some of the female bustards greeted us as we entered the paddock and took a largesse of bread from our hands, preening themselves and dropping lovely feathers like autumn leaves, which we triumphantly wore in our hats. In spite of careful protection, the numbers of this magnificent bird continue to decline. It is particularly vulnerable since it nests in a depression in the open ground of the steppe and so makes its eggs and young an easy target for predators, including such merciless predators as ploughs and tractors.

The llamas (right) in their rather posh get-up of white shirt and dark trousers wandered about the landscape wearing that affronted look that this creature always assumes. Hailing from the high Andes, it is not surprising that the llama adapts well to the cold conditions of the steppes, but it was surprising to see that the nilgai (below), from the hot plains of India, had taken to this inimical climate so well.

The markhor (far right) with its solemn face and extraordinary horns twisted like old-fashioned sticks of barley sugar, is one of the largest members of the goat family and comes from the vast mountain ranges of Central Asia.

disputing the rights to his territory. He lowered his wings and spread his tail like a peacock, with a crisp rustle of feathers like someone undoing a starched shirt, and attacked the sack with his heavy beak, like the magnified beak of a chicken, biting and twisting the cloth, uttering reverberating drumming (or rather thrumming) noises deep in his chest, in an impressive display of ferocity. More people, of course, mean more agricultural land needed and in consequence less room for the bustard. However, one hopes there will still be corners where this magnificent and beautiful bird will be allowed to decorate our planet.

After we had finished being entranced by the bustards, we piled into jeeps and made our way out to the area of steppe land on which the cloven-hoofed and other large mammals were kept. Here in these vast paddocks were herds of Indian nilgai, American buffalo — ·hunched, black and curly — and parti-coloured llamas that looked as though they

Left: The wonderful aristocratic and elegant eland is a great feature of Askaniya Nova, where a sensible attempt is being made to domesticate it. This beautiful beast may well – in future years – replace cattle in tropical countries.
It was interesting to note that while the North American bison (centre right) flourished at Askaniya Nova, being an animal of the prairie, no success had been had with the European species, which is forest loving.

Below: Like all the various forms of wild ass in the world, the handsome kulan is in danger of extinction throughout its range. However, with strict conservation measures, its numbers are increasing and it has even been successfully reintroduced into Central Asia.

The Przewalski's horse, once so common, was only saved from extinction by breeding in zoos. It is now about to be re-introduced into its former range in Mongolia using captive-bred animals. The cousin of this horse, the tarpan, used to live on the steppes but is now extinct. Let us hope that, through wise conservation, the Przewalski's horse does not follow it.

were wearing white shirts and chocolate-coloured trousers. There were herds of brindled gnu, ballet dancing over the grass and uttering purring grunts, and large groups of eland, aristocratic-looking, feeding with the boisterous gnu in a very well-behaved fashion. The two animals that interested me most were the wild ass, or kulan, and the Przewalski's or Mongolian wild horse. The kulan flashed past us, their sleek coats gleaming in the sun, their dark manes like carefully plaited pigtails down their necks, ran parallel with us for a time and then swerved off and were soon lost to view. The kulan is very rare in the Soviet Union now, but they are breeding well in Askaniya Nova.

The Mongolian wild horses are fine dun-coloured stocky animals with somewhat elongated faces that give them a faintly Chinese cast of countenance. They have dark manes and resemble a Welsh pony from a distance. The young are a pale cream colour when they are born and only attain the adult coloration when they are two years old. These nice little horses were first found by the great Russian explorer Przewalski in the last century. Once common, the animals gradually dwindled in numbers in the face of the spread of agriculture and competition from domestic animals. Now they are thought to be extinct in the wild (though recent rumour has it that a small herd may still exist), but fortunately some had found their way into various zoological collections in Russia, Europe and America, where they bred well and prospered. So well have they done, in fact, that while we were in Askaniya Nova, there was a conference being held in Moscow attended by representatives from American zoos, some European zoos and that most remarkable of English zoos, Marwell, where a huge herd of these horses is kept. The object of the exercise was to work out joint plans for returning the Mongolian wild horse to a suitable area in Mongolia, using captive-bred animals from all over the world. We do not seem to have much success in getting international cooperation in the arms race – let's see if we can get it for the Mongolian wild horse.

There were two herds of horses, one consisting of an old stallion, some ten or twelve mares and their pale babies, and the other of a group of about six bachelor males. On our second day when we were out filming we saw an example of just how savage the battles among these horses can be. Before we arrived, one of the bachelor stallions, fed up with his lonely state, had decided to tackle the old stallion for supremacy over the mares. I don't know how long they had been fighting, but they were both black and shining with sweat. There were great bites on both their flanks and shoulders, gushing blood that bespattered the grass as they galloped to and fro, squealing, kicking and biting, while all the time travelling at top speed. The mares and foals seemed bewildered by all this savagery, and milled about distractedly, now running one way, now another, as the sweating, bloodstained stallions wheeled around them. It seemed that there would be no end to the fight, for neither stallion would give in, and until one dropped dead from exhaustion they had reached a gory impasse. However, at that moment, one of the rangers saw what was happening and galloped over on his horse, wielding a long bull whip. With its aid, he managed to play referee to the two animals and finally succeeded in driving the intrusive stallion, bloody but unbowed, back to the bachelor herd.

That afternoon we filmed some of the other activities of Askaniya Nova. As well as breeding rare animals like the Mongolian horse and the kulan, they breed commoner animals like ostrich, South American rheas and Australian emus, with which they supply other Soviet zoos. This is an excellent scheme, for all zoos should aim, through their breeding, to become self-sufficient, thus not becoming a constant drain on ever-diminishing wild stocks. First we filmed the ostrich, with their elegant plumes and great ballet dancer's thighs, and they behaved beautifully. Then we went into a large paddock containing a father emu and his brood of some eleven chicks. The father emu was a spirited bird and it was obvious that he did not take kindly to this intrusion of his privacy. Paul, when busy directing, sometimes went

Ostriches are most peculiar birds, both in appearance and in manner, with their great naked thighs like dancers in a corps de ballet, their huge, dreamy eyes and their beaks wearing a shy smirk.

The emu is the Australian counterpart of the ostrich. Their rather ridiculous appearance belies the fact that they can disembowel you with a swift downward kick, and that is just what one attempted to do to our director. Here (right) is the protective father making up his mind to charge when we got too close to his brood.

Opposite: The orderly circle of eland we had been led to expect did not materialize. To the chagrin of their milkmaids, they behaved in the most unruly fashion (above). Finally, after much effort, we got one to stand still long enough to be milked (inset). Lee was almost overwhelmed by baby eland (bottom). The bucket of milk being empty, they started to suck her fingers in an attempt to obtain more sustenance, and eventually backed her up against the fence so that we had to go and rescue her.

into a trance in which he became oblivious to everything but the film, and so he was unaware of the malevolent looks the emu kept darting at him. When he proposed that the camera should once more be moved closer to the babies, the father emu decided he had had enough, and he rightly singled out Paul as being the ringleader of these troublesome humans. Before anyone could do anything sensible or shout a warning, he had put on a sudden burst of speed, rushed up to Paul and kicked him smartly in the crutch. Now both the 'stars' and the crew have frequently felt the urge to kick a director in the crutch, but have lacked the moral courage (I have, at any rate). It took one of our feathered friends to show us how it should be done. We were caught, as it were, between horror and a wild desire to laugh. A kick from any of these heavy flightless birds can be most dangerous and, in fact, an ostrich can disembowel you with a well directed blow from its clawed foot. We shooed the still indignant emu away before he could have another go at the same target and clustered round our noble director to review the damage. Fortunately, the emu's aim had not been true and while aiming for the crutch he had miscalculated and hit him on the thigh, painful enough but not so disastrous. I told Paul I was disappointed as I had always wanted to be directed by a boy soprano, and he gave me a very icy look.

We next went to film the milking of the eland herd. This is one of the most interesting studies being undertaken at Askaniya Nova for basically what they are trying to do is to domesticate this huge, elegant antelope, for it provides not only quantities of excellent meat, but rich and valuable milk as well. In fact, an ingredient of eland's milk had been found to help cure tuberculosis, gastric ulcers and wounds that do not heal. From the conservation point of view it would be much to the land's benefit to have herds of domesticated eland (a selective feeder) roaming over the savannas of Africa rather than the scrawny herds of erosive cows. In addition, the eland (apart from being more beautiful to look at than a cow) is immune to tsetse fly, whereas the cow is not. The experiments to domesticate the eland could have far reaching effects in the future for agriculture in tropical countries.

We were told that the eland were brought out of their stables and taken out into one of the huge steppe enclosures. Here they would stand in a sedate circle to be milked and then go off to the fragrant

Crossing the steppe in the early morning was a magical experience, for the whole intricate world of plants and animals was just coming to life. The horses' hooves kicked up fountains of dew and the smell of the crushed grasses and flowers was overwhelming.

steppe to graze. Furthermore, we were told, they were extremely nervous, so we should avoid sudden movements and noise. We agreed to all these strictures, set up the camera tiptoeing around the steppe, speaking in hushed whispers and generally doing our best not to upset the delicate nervous system of our stars. Then came the magic moment when the two ladies in charge of the herd emerged, carrying buckets to milk into, milking stools, buckets of corn to keep their charges happy and, as a special treat, buckets of bread. All these were carefully arranged in a row. There was a moment's hushed silence and then the gates were opened.

We had mentally prepared ourselves for a two-hour wait before the elands would appear. We imagined them peering timidly round the gate, gazing at us, terrified, retreating to their stable until they had plucked up courage to attempt once more to venture out, slowly, delicately, starting at every sound, shying at every shadow, trembling bundles of nerves. Nothing, it turned out, could have been further from the truth. As the gates were opened, like children let out of school, this herd of immense and beautiful creatures came dashing out into the paddock, their eyes alight with interest. They knocked over the pails of corn, they kicked over the milking stools, they stole loaves of bread and ran away with them, they came and breathed on the camera so that the lens fogged up and generally behaved so badly that it was some little time before their 'milkmaids' could get them under control. With considerable effort and much bribery with the bread they had not already pillaged, we got them into what could, with imagination, be described as a circle. By this time, of course, they were thoroughly over-excited and in consequence most of them would not give milk. They were too busy kicking each other, prodding each other with their handsome cornucopia-like horns and stealing each other's bread. Eventually we managed to get a tiny dribble of milk from one of them, but it was obvious that appearing on television had thoroughly demoralized them. The following day, however, they behaved properly and yielded a large jug of milk, which we chilled in the refrigerator and later drank. It was delicious, thick and creamy and

On every side as far as the eye could see spiders' webs gleamed.

As the sun rose and lifted the mist like a stage curtain, various actors of the steppe made their appearance: the Bobac marmots (above left), rare now on the steppe, look as portly as well-paid aldermen; the tiny map toads (above), their skin an atlas of greens, reds and fawns; and the handsomely marked viper (left), ready for the day, his back marked like black lighting.

The rising sun made the delicate feather grass glisten and the other flower colours glow. The feather grass (an endangered species) is found nowhere except on the steppes and this is probably its last stronghold.

There are 450 species of plants on this virgin steppe but they are as ephemeral as snow – a brief blaze of colour in the spring and then the sun bleaches the whole steppe to yellow, the flowers dead, the grass as crisp as toast. One of our favourites was like a tiny flat-topped acacia burdened with the title of Goniolimon tataricum *(opposite), such a ponderous name to give to such a beautiful plant.*

slightly sweet. It would be wonderful if eland could be domesticated if for no other reason than they would put beauty into our domestic breeds, for they are magnificent beasts.

On our final day we went out to the large area of virgin steppe that has been preserved. Here you are not allowed to go in anything other than horse and trap (and then only in certain areas) or on foot, for it really is as it was before the coming of man with all his destructive influence. We wanted to see and film the Bobak marmots, large handsome rodents, which at one time were common here but had become extinct. Several reintroductions had been tried and all failed until the last one 'took'.

We set off in the trap at sunrise. We had travelled perhaps a mile, and soon we could hear the piping alarm calls of the marmots, for though we could not see them – nor they us – they could hear our approach. When we got close to their burrows we abandoned the trap and moved cautiously forward. As the sun warmed the mist, the steppe started to come alive. Mantids, moths, butterflies and spiders drying out from their night's dew-drenched sleep started to move amongst the resplendent tapestry of flowers.

Suddenly the sun pulled up the curtain of mist near us, and there was the marmot township and, sitting at the door of one of the burrows, its fat, prosperous owner, a handsome creature, a rich chestnut-brown on the back and with a pale yellow tummy. He was soon joined by his mate and they both sat bolt upright regarding us with suspicion. However, as we made no move they soon relaxed and started feeding. Presently their babies emerged and started to feed, clean their faces and occasionally break off from these important duties to practise a little judo. We watched and filmed this enchanting family for some time and then, with reluctance, we retraced our way over the steppe, feeling we ought to bend down and apologise to the inhabitants of each plant for our Gulliver-like intrusion into their small, fragrant and brilliantly coloured world.

Nick Drozdov joined us at Askaniya Nova, and on the last day we had a picnic on the warm, flower-scented virgin steppe where the insects were having a feast among the blooms around us. For once Nick had not got his Gladstone bag full of presents with him, but just having him with us in such enchanting surroundings was present enough.

CAUCASUS
Return of the bison

КАВКАЗ
CAUCASUS

After our frozen sojourn in the mountains it was wonderful to experience the warmth of Tbilisi, the capital of Georgia, where in the market you could buy such exotic fruit as pomegranates, red as winter suns and sweet as honey.

ONE of our first sorties outside Moscow was to the breeding station for European bison. The history of this majestical animal is an excellent example of how a species can be saved from extinction by captive breeding. At one time the bison was found throughout the forests of Europe and Russia but gradually, owing to overhunting and the destruction of its habitat, its numbers dwindled until the only wild herd to be found at the beginning of this century was in the Bialowieza Forest in eastern Poland and in the foothills of the Caucasus. The horrors of the First World War and its aftermath killed off the remaining wild bison by the 1920s. Fortunately, however, there was a captive stock of these fine animals and in 1923 a society was formed for the protection and breeding of the bison. Gradually the numbers increased, and in the 1950s bison were returned to the Bialowieza Forest. The Soviet Union decided that the animal ought to be reintroduced into the southern parts of its former range as well, and so a breeding centre outside Moscow was set up in the 1940s under the guidance of Dr Michael Zablotsky.

We drove out to the centre through miles and miles of snow-drenched birch forest. They were massive trees, their delicate, leafless branches curving over, fountain-like against the skyline, like black lace, their huge silver trunks, blotched with black (no two the same – like fingerprints), looking like the skins of a million dalmatians in the snow. It was intensely cold but with a pale blue sky and sunshine that made the birches' satiny bark shine as if freshly lacquered. The few conifers we passed were dark baize-green, wearing muffs of snow on their branches. At the reserve, we were met by Dr Zablotsky and his daughter, Marina, who explained the breeding programme to us. Five hundred acres of a 12,000-acre nature reserve are set aside for bison breeding. There are seventy animals kept as breeding stock, and the offspring are shipped to the Caucasus or the Carpathians when they are about two years old. They join other two-year-olds from other breeding stations in the Soviet Union, and are released in small herds in the late summer. A forest ranger is detailed to follow and observe them to see how they get on in their first winter. There are about 1000 wild bison now in the Soviet mountains, thanks to this breeding and release programme.

We then went out to the paddocks to see the bison, or wisent, which is its ancient name. It was nice to see, in an adjoining paddock, a small herd of American bison, so that we could make comparisons between the two species. The American bison are burly beasts, with high, humped shoulders covered with curly hair, and wide and massive heads. In contrast, the European bison, being forest instead of prairie animals, are more slender and streamlined, with longer legs and not nearly such bulky heads and shoulders. We went into the paddock with

Preceding page: The Caucasus Mountains and (inset) the European bison.

64

them and, although slightly wary, they allowed us to approach within ten or twelve feet of them as they stood chewing hay, sighing deeply and heavily and scrunching their hooves in the crisp snow as they moved. Occasionally, one of them would utter a subdued gurgling cry, like the moo of a semi-strangulated domestic cow suffering from severe laryngitis. Lee, intrigued, asked if there was any difference between the vocalization of this bison and its American cousin.

'Not much difference,' said Marina, 'except that the European ones are more gloomy.' It conjured up a vision of the bison as one of those doomed heroes in some of the more depressing and introspective Russian novels in which everyone seems to end up committing suicide in the barn. After we had admired the small herd in the smaller paddock, we went to the larger herd in a paddock of about 125 acres. They, of course, had vanished deep into the forest, but presently a very rotund pink and white lady made her appearance, carrying a large brass trumpet. With puffed cheeks and frowning brow, she blew a series of echoing and sonorous blasts on the instrument and soon — fortunately before she was overcome with musical apoplexy — the bison appeared, drifting languidly through the trees, snorting hopefully at the promise of food.

The young bison are caught up in special crates and loaded onto huge long-distance lorries, which transport them some 2000 miles to the wild mountainous region of the Caucasus. To accompany the bison on their mammoth journey to freedom would have taken far too long in our tight schedule, so we went ahead, flying down to Sochi on the Black Sea coast, a fine holiday town which, because of its excellent

The Soviet Union has met with great success in breeding the European bison and in reintroducing it to parts of its former range. Picnicking in a forest and having these magnificent beasts join you would be an immense privilege, even if it meant climbing a tree while it ate your sandwiches.

The difference between the American and European bison is very apparent when you see them side by side: the American animal (right) is much more burly, with heavier shoulders and a more massive head, whereas the European species (opposite) is a more slender and graceful-looking creature.

Animals bred here just outside Moscow are transported thousands of miles to the wilds of the Caucasus and Carpathian Mountains to form new wild herds.

We travelled to the Caucasus Mountains to see how this reintroduction scheme for the bison was faring.

climate, is known as the Riviera of the Soviet Union. Here we and our mountainous pile of equipment were crushed into a huge chopper with four pilots that flew us thirty miles into the mountains. We were joined here by Anatoly, the chief ranger, who was to be our guide. A massive man with a huge infectious grin, his job was to spend weeks alone in the mountains carrying, as it were, his home on his back like a snail, studying the animals in the reserve. He viewed us all with benign amusement as if we were all slightly mentally retarded children. His English was miniscule but spoken with such enthusiasm you could grasp his point. 'Lee, John,' he would groan, when we lit up cigarettes, 'don't shmoke, don't shmoke, shmoking *bad*.'

It was a magnificent flight, since we did not go too high and so could appreciate the scenery. The mountains were covered with a rug of trees, green, yellow, scarlet and orange, but their bare tops were scarfed and beribboned with snow. From carved rocky outcrops, waterfalls drifted like skeins of white lawn, and in the fields we could see the amber glint of rivers and the occasional mirror-like flash of a mountain lake. Groups of doves flew below us in hundreds, like handfuls of confetti flung across the valleys. We landed at last in a handsome valley, where our chopper blades blew the dead leaves off the poplars like a shower of gold coins. We settled into our quarters – a large stone guest house, with huge, freezing-cold bedrooms and a cavernous living room mercifully made warm by a gigantic log fire. Here we thawed out, for the chopper had no heating and we were numb with cold.

The gear was unpacked and we set off once more in the chopper in

search of bison. We flew higher and higher into the mountains, where above the tree line great snowfields glittered like sugar in the sun. Suddenly, the chopper dropped and banked and we saw the pilot had spotted six chamois bouncing puppet-like through the snow and rocks as though they were on strings, their horns like back-to-front question marks on the top of their heads. Ten minutes later we found four wild goats, turs, as they are called here. They were not nearly as agile as the chamois but were very handsome creatures with long, curved horns like heavy scimitars. This was all very exciting and with cameras and binoculars we rushed from side to side in the chopper, shouting instructions and information to each other, which everyone disregarded.

Then we turned to head for home, disappointed that we had not seen any bison, but after half an hour, we flew over an enormous hillside patched with snow and right in the middle of it was what looked at first glance like a large outcrop of brown rocks. However, our pilot zoomed down towards it and we soon saw that it was a galloping herd of some thirty bison, brown as chestnuts. Hastily, our pilot put the chopper down and we tumbled out on to the snow to pursue the bison and try to film them. The snow was knee deep, which hampered us but did not hamper the animals, who had longer legs. We pursued them, gasping and panting, for the altitude was affecting us, and at last came to a steep, bare rise that allowed us to get some shots of them as they galloped off, but we could not follow them. So, satisfied with our day, we flew home to a large vodka-irrigated meal.

The next day, because we wanted to try to see and film tur from the

When we reached the mountains, we continued our journey by helicopter across some of the most stunning landscapes I had ever seen.

Overleaf: *Suddenly we had our first glimpse of the wild bison, galloping up a steep slope. It was amazing to watch as we were gasping and panting at that altitude, whereas the bison, like a black bed of coals, swept up the hillside like woolly express trains.* Inset: *Carved in the snow are the busy auto routes of the mountain animals, all converging on the essential place of pleasure, the salt lick (*left*). On the higher slopes we could see chamois bouncing along (*centre*). The tur or Caucasian ibex (*right*) is one member of the goat family we hoped to see, and we went high into the mountains to visit its domain. Finally, to our delight, we saw the tur moving along a snowfield, sure-footed and somewhat heraldic-looking creatures.*

Above and opposite: *Travelling by jeep to look for tur, we stopped at a bee farm, where the owner insisted we wear bee veils to protect us from the attention of his charges. As we climbed higher and higher we found firs and larches draped with frozen, hanging lichens, and leaves edged with ice from the biting wind.*

ground, we set off up the mountains in a couple of jeeps. In the lower reaches the oaks and beeches were golden and yellow, the leaves fluttering and pirouetting down to land in our hair and on our laps, crisp as biscuits. We drove for some way along a broad, shallow, amber-coloured river that had white manes of water round each polished rock, and then we came to a remote valley full of apple trees and under them a veritable metropolis of wooden beehives, painted blue, yellow and grey. We stopped to film it, and the owner brought out a great pot of honey – looking as though filled with molten gold – and spooned it out onto a plate for us to eat. It was simply delicious. Then the bee-owner loaded us up with yellow apples, so twisted and misshapen that they would have made even Snow White suspicious, but they tasted crisp and sweet.

As we got higher, the firs and larches began, their branches draped in greeny-grey lichens like Spanish moss, which the wind blew to and fro like curtains, but as we got higher still, the lichens were immobile under a layer of ice. You could tell the prevailing direction of the wind by the white rim of ice along the edges of the branches, and each leaf of the bushes was rimmed with ice crystals like feathers on a bird's wing. When we got to 6000 feet we were above the clouds and could watch them pouring into the valleys like cream being poured into green and gold bowls. Here the snow was falling in the shape of pinhead-sized snowballs and the silence was so intense you could hear them pattering on the snow beneath the trees. It was terribly cold and so we lit a huge fire and roasted shish kebabs and sausages over it and drank gallons of tea. I had stupidly left my hat behind and, intensely protective of my welfare, Anatoly insisted on making me wear his huge sheepskin hat, for which I was most grateful, as it was like wearing a

Eventually the road burst through its misty shroud and we reached the heights. At this altitude we could look down and see the clouds moving into the valleys like cream (opposite), and up to the glaciers held fast in the arms of the mountains (left). It was so silent we could actually hear the snow falling, and so cold that we were glad of a fire and some hot tea. I was very grateful to Anatoly for lending me a hat to keep my head warm (inset opposite).

brazier on your head. Presently we went higher still to the next zone, where the trees suddenly retreated and their place was taken by miniature rhododendrons, each leaf striped with snow. Beyond this zone were the snowfields and the huge, carunculated outcrops of rock. This was the kingdom of the tur and chamois and the snow grouse. We saw snow grouse (or, to be strictly accurate, Anatoly, without binoculars, saw them and I, with binoculars, could not see them) and suddenly there was a tur, silhouetted on the crest of a snow field, standing arrogant and majestic, with his horns thrown back. Presently he was joined by another and the two of them moved along the rim of the snow field, walking slowly and pausing to gaze down at us with disdain. We watched and filmed them for a time and then the clouds started to shoulder into the mountains and we were – in film parlance – losing light, so we started on the downward journey through flurries of snow and banks of cloud that enveloped us like freezing smoke.

The next day we were picked up by the chopper and winged off through the mountains, each one with a cloud impaled on its summit. From on high the mountains looked like a gigantic unmade bed, covered with a bearskin quilt in brown, red and gold. Eventually we arrived at Psluch, where we were to film the home of a typical forester. We found an excellent camp site laid out for the crew but, to our embarrassment, we found that Lee and I were to stay with the forester, Victor, and his wife, Natasha. I say to our embarrassment because their whole house consisted of two rooms, a bedroom and a living room, with a huge wood burning stove in it, and they had moved out of their bedroom and made up two featherbeds for us, while they slept in the living room – they would not hear of any other arrangement. They were an enchanting couple – Natasha with her gamin face, across which kaleidoscopic expressions chased, her twenty words of English more than aided and abetted by her expressive hands and her skill at mimicry, while Victor, handsome, bearded, looking like some elegant conquistador, smiling benignly, making sure that our glasses were filled at all times, and then astonishing us by stating gravely during a pause in the conversation, 'Gerry, I luff you', apropos of nothing we had

Eventually, at the very crest of the mountains, Anatoly spotted some Caucasian ibex, eking out a hard existence in their bleak mountain stronghold.

been talking about. They both had been actors and had taken part in a number of Soviet films, but then had decided that life in the bustling city of Odessa was too restricted, and so they had applied for and got this job. Their tiny house was crammed with their possessions, books, pictures, photographs, and exuded an air of warmth, cosiness and the bright intelligences that inhabited it.

We had a splendid if slightly inebriated evening, talking about their animal pets – which ranged from bear to chamois – with Natasha doing imitations of them all. Then we tumbled into our warm, comfortable beds and slept like the dead until dawn, when we went through into the living room to discover Natasha, who had obviously been up for several hours, preparing breakfast, a repast fit for royalty. They had unearthed their great-grandmother's silver-plated samovar, a huge, heavily-decorated urn-like object that dominated the breakfast table. I had, in my ignorance, always thought that you made tea in the samovar, but you don't. It is simply a hot water dispenser, the glowing coals inside it making sure that you have hot water for tea-making at all times. As well as tea there was fresh milk (warm from their cow), two types of yoghurt-like soured cream (one very sour and one sweetish), goat cheese, cakes, scones (freshly baked), honey, fresh walnuts and tiny wild pears preserved in syrup. It was all so delicious that we behaved like gluttons.

We were extremely sorry to have to leave Victor and Natasha, for they were a warm and charming couple, but now we had to chopper back to Sochi and take the train to Georgia, where we hoped to film the to and fro migration up the mountains, for with the coming of spring, wild animals and birds move up the mountains, accompanied by domestic flocks of sheep, cows and goats and even beehives, and then with the first snows they all come down to the lowlands. However, on our arrival at Tbilisi we found that winter weather had started early and all the flocks had been forced down from the mountains, so we had to sit in the town for five days, filming in the most magnificent market and in the enchanting back streets of the town, where each house had

beautiful ornately carved balconies, painted blue, green or gold.

Then, exhausted, we flew back to Moscow. A note in my diary says: 'It's extraordinary how quickly you can tire of red caviar. A steady diet of this soon makes you feel like a dyspeptic snooker player.'

Flying past the mountains with their peaks rising through the clouds.

A handsome snow grouse.

ASTRAKHAN & KALMYK
Cormorants, crows and catfish

АСТРАХАНЬ И КАЛМЫЦКАЯ _{А.С.С.Р.}

ASTRAKHAN & KALMYK

As we started our wonderful trip down the Volga, the ripples from our wake disturbed many different insects, like dragonflies, who purred past us on shiny wings.

THE great reserve of Astrakhan that embraces a large portion of the Volga delta is of particular importance both biologically and historically. Lenin, a far-sighted man, was a great believer in conservation in an age when conservation was only beginning to be taken seriously as a concept. In 1918 you would have thought that Lenin would have had quite enough on his plate without worrying about nature reserves. But for many years the Volga delta had been overfished and the enormous bird population decimated by feather poachers and their eggs stolen to manufacture soap. The Astrakhan authorities approached Lenin with a plan – a very intelligent plan – for creating a huge reserve in the lush reaches of the Volga where it spreads out, like the fingers of a hand, to embrace the Caspian Sea. Lenin immediately saw the necessity for this and so the Astrakhan Reserve, which we were now to visit, was the first reserve created in the Soviet Union.

Taking the plane from Moscow at ten at night, we arrived in Astrakhan in a frowsty and irritable state at two in the morning. However, after a sleep, my bad mood disappeared, for we were again in one of those cities of magical names that I had only read about in my youth and had longed to visit. As it turned out, we had little chance to appreciate its charms other than driving through it on our way to the river, but it seemed a comfortable, elderly town, with nice clapboard houses and tasteful wood carving on the shutters and lintels. Most towns in the Soviet Union are brash, big and half-finished. Why, one asked oneself, did the people want to live in anything other than these charming wooden houses? I can't believe that anyone would willingly exchange one of these lovely buildings with their fairytale look for a hideous highrise flat that has less artistic appeal than a dustbin.

Finally we reached the banks of the Volga and there our little fleet awaited us – two eighty-foot long barges with elegant awnings and seats and tables for dining on deck, and below, two comfortable double cabins and a single one. There was a small saloon in which you could dine if the inclemencies of the weather made it impossible to eat out on deck. It was luxurious and we felt as though the *Queen Elizabeth II* had been put at our disposal. It was a great thrill to be travelling down the Volga – certainly not the longest river in the Soviet Union but one that, over the years, has collected more press coverage than any other, and so is better known. And what an elegant, varied and beautiful river it was.

To begin with the river was wide and a curious shade of browny-green. The banks were wooded and here and there we could see the lovely little wooden houses, all with gaily painted shutters, and here and there a small factory with an important-looking cloud of smoke coming from its chimneys. Then, as we started to reach more

Preceding page: The cormorant colony and (inset) a baby saiga – less than two weeks after birth it can run at 50 miles an hour.

80

open country the aspect of the river changed. Here was green pastureland, and the river rim – extra-high because of flood water – was guarded by ranks of huge ancient willows, fat as dowager duchesses, their great tummies striped and fretted as if by too tight corset marks, standing up to their knees in water. Below them was a wide bank of reeds, stiff and upright, each with its white plume, so that they looked like an army going into battle. The boat ahead of us raised a smooth green muscle of water that curved and rippled like some dragon's tail and slapped into the army of reeds making them tremble, rustle and bend, disturbing flocks of glitter-winged dragonflies that zoomed, quivered and shone in the still air. In places behind the reed beds, behind the corpulent willows, there were acres and acres of tamarisk in bloom, a most beautiful dusky pink. I asked why the tamarisk trees were only knee high, thinking they might be a different species from the Mediterranean ones I was familiar with, but it turned out that these tamarisk forests were so dwarfed because the local people cut the trees for firewood. I have always been fond of tamarisks, and to see such sheets of these mini-trees in bloom, like great pink counterpanes, was a really splendid sight. In places where the grass was very tall and lush it was obviously frog-filled and a favourite hunting ground for egrets and herons, dozens of which stalked along looking disembodied, since only their long necks and heads were visible above the high grass. As we progressed in a slow and stately manner down the river the stands of ancient willow grew thicker and were stuffed with rookeries, thousands of nests like strange black fruit in the greenery, and there was such a cacophonous chorus from the birds that the air throbbed as if one were passing a giant's beehive.

Our large boat was majestic and ploughed its way through the waters, passing banks that there alive with insects and birds.

Gulls (top left) *and terns* (above) *abounded, filling the air with their cries. Great egrets* (top right) *prowled the moist meadows ready to spear the unwary frog or fish.*

Opposite: *The house* (top) *where we stayed was surrounded by flooded meadows that pulsated with a chorus of frogs and was brilliant with dragonflies. As we explored the reedbeds that surrounded us* (centre left), *we found numerous water birds' nests, some with eggs, some with forlorn-looking young like this purple heron chick* (bottom left). *On the overhanging branches were many Penduline tits' nests* (bottom centre), *posssibly the most comfy-looking cradles for eggs and young in the bird world. In the trees, looking bright as though newly scrubbed, rollers* (bottom right) *were busy about the task of gathering food for their young. At one point a wild boar* (centre right) *foraging in the shallows for roots, snails, birds' nests and other edible trifles, was panicked by our sudden appearance.*

Caspian terns, delicate as giant butterflies, etched the green surface of the water with their beaks as they fed. Birds of all sorts and shapes were now appearing in numbers. Great black-headed gulls, brilliant black and white with a curious round pale mark on the forewing like a fingerprint, flew over us with a strong, lunging, impatient flight like an American businessman on his way to a lucrative merger.

Eventually we turned off the main river and travelled down a narrower tributary, and here the birds became even more prolific. The air was thick with them: cuckoos, hawk-like, dashing busily through the willows; every dead stump decorated with the brilliant plumage of a roller; herons with their heavy sedate flight; terns, crows and swallows skimming the reeds in search of the insect bounty that our wake was disturbing. After travelling for several miles through this bewildering ornithological firework display, we came eventually to the reserve headquarters in a nicely laid out tiny village, and we were given a little house to live in, set in a watery meadow full of frogs calling like petulant small children. We settled in and for the next three days had one of the most wonderful times I have had in my life, for not only was the reserve marvellously beautiful, but it was also so rich in all forms of life, overflowing with such an abundance that we were hard-pressed at times to know what to look at.

We explored and filmed the various waterways and creeks that lay in an intricate network around us, using a fleet of small boats with outboard engines. The motors were used only to take us to a given point and were then switched off so we drifted gently with the current. As we set off in the mornings we would drift down the narrow sparkling channels of tawny water, close to the whispering reed beds, which had here and there hung in them Penduline tits' nests like miniature Victorian muffs, delicate oval constructions of feathers and soft fluff from the reed heads. The architects of these graceful nests were attractive, delicate little birds with rusty-red shoulders and a prominent black bandit's mask across the eyes, and they flicked and danced through the reeds like tiny acrobats. The reed beds were full of dragonflies, large, blue as delphiniums, flying in honeymoon tandem, passing us in a frosty glitter of wings. In the waters by the reeds the wash from our boats made the green plate leaves of the waterlilies bob up and down and sent the sage-green frogs skittering across them, and in the shallow places the fish fry lay, gently moving, so closely packed

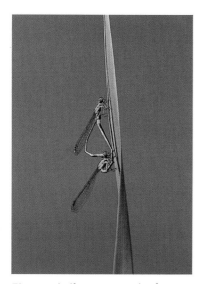

The way to the cormorant colony was lined with reed beds, where damselflies were engaged in a frenzy of mating. Cormorant parents fly once or twice a day to the mouth of the delta or even beyond into the Caspian Sea to fish for their families.

they looked like a brown lace veil carelessly cast into the water. In the shallows the damselflies, burnished bronze and blue as forget-me-nots, were busy egg-laying. The males stood upright on their wives' heads while the poor females hovered over the water dipping their tails in to deposit eggs on the underside of fallen bullrush stalks. It is a most complex method of reproduction, for it is as if you were asked to give birth to quintuplets while levitating with your husband standing on your head.

Our ultimate destination was a cormorant colony, and as the creeks narrowed, we could hear the uproar of the cormorants in the trees ahead. These are the great cormorants, handsome shining black birds with yellow round the eye and the base of the beak, white cheeks and a slight grizzle of white on the head and upper neck. This colony numbers 1200 pairs, but in the whole of the Astrakhan Reserve there are a hundred thousand individuals. Rodney went ahead in the other boat and we allowed our craft to drift on the current, which carried us right down until we bumped gently into a log jam right in the centre of the colony. It was a stupendous sight. Everywhere among the half-dead trees, each painted white by the birds' droppings, were huge stick nests, some about two feet thick and three or four feet across. They were placed very close together, in some places touching, and in each one sat the baby cormorants – at this stage fully fledged – waiting for their parents to come and feed them. Many nests had only two babies in them, but quite a lot had up to four. They sat in the blazing sun, their throats pulsing as they panted, uttering plaintive tweeting noises. As the parent birds did not all go to sea together, mothers or fathers were always arriving with cropfuls of fish for the young, so the whole colony was constantly in movement. As the parent bird appeared, the babies would spot it some distance away (though how they recognized it was a mystery, for all the adults looked identical to me), and their plaintive tweeting would change to loud wheezing cries as the parent arrived at the nest. As the parent bird landed it would utter a loud brassy trumpeting cry, and the babies with trembling

As well as being strong fliers, cormorants are excellent swimmers and divers, pursuing fish under water. On or by the nests the young ones sat and panted in the hot sun, waiting for their parents to return with food.

To be in the midst of such a huge conglomeration of birds is an extraordinary experience, for the air vibrates with cries and the sound of wings and in this avian city nothing is ever still. Here and there our eye would be caught by the little egrets (right), gleaming like snowdrop buds. The night heron (far right) in its black hook, hunched as a hanging judge, is not above pillaging other birds' nests to provide its own young with sustenance.

The glossy ibis (right), with feathers like shot silk, laid her eggs in a well-concealed nest, and overhead the spoonbills (far right), with their extraordinary beaks like elongated ping-pong bats, flew back to their nests, their wings lazily beating the hot air.

wings would solicit, banging their beaks against their parent's to get it to regurgitate. Under this stimulus the parent would suddenly open its beak, whereupon the baby would plunge its head inside to gobble up the warm slush of semi-digested fish the parent brought up.

We spent many hours at this idyllic spot, watching the cormorants and other birds (for dotted about the colony were nests of herons, glossy ibis, cattle egrets, hooded crows, woodpeckers and a host of others), and talking to the resident ornithologists about the cormorants' undeserved reputation on the delta. The fishermen in the Caspian Sea complained about the cormorants, saying that they ate too many fish and their excrement burnt the trees and killed them. However, careful investigations were made and a wonderful pattern began to emerge. It was discovered that the cormorant was beneficial, not detrimental, to the delta – in fact, without them there would be fewer fish, not more. What happens is this. The birds arrive to breed just as the floods are moving down the Volga, pushing a great mass of water through the delta and into the Caspian Sea. The cormorants' excrement, rich in nitrogen and phosphorus, is swept down and fertilizes the whole delta area in which the fish fry live, providing more food for them in the shallows and fertilizing the banks. Moreover, it is

The parent cormorant pauses before feeding its eager young while a hooded crow waits patiently for its chance to terrify the young into regurgitating their food (above left). The crow itself and the huge menacing catfish (above) waiting for titbits in the waters below benefit from this banditry, illustrating how the cormorant is a vital link in the ecology of the delta.

Cormorants return from fishing, like a line of ebony crosses in the sky.

A little later in the summer the open water would be covered with the famous lotuses, like an orchestra of green trumpets, and in the shallows would be sedate green nosegays of water chestnuts.

thought that the cormorants are not responsible for destroying the trees. They choose elderly trees at the end of their life span for preference; after two or three years the tree dies naturally and while it stands the birds continue to nest in it.

A curious relationship we noticed as we watched the colony was the unlikely association between crows and fish. In the shallow amber waters below the cormorants' nests swam huge catfish, four to five feet long, heads six to eight inches across, huge sulky faces and large moustaches of long barbels. In the upper branches of the trees lurked, bandit-like, hooded crows. These highly intelligent birds had worked out a successful system of mugging. As soon as a parent cormorant had fed its babies and flown off, the crows would fly down to the nest and converge on the babies. A couple of well-placed, intimidating pecks and the young cormorants would regurgitate their food in fright. Some of the fish fell in the nest and this the crows stole, but the rest fell through the branches and into the water to be immediately sucked into the pouting mouths of the catfish.

The Astrakhan Reserve was a fascinating place and we could have spent weeks there, for every day we saw something new. In the central channel the to-ing and fro-ing was endless. Cormorants by the score, like strings of ebony crosses, flicked across the sky; stately, slow-flying herons, with heads and necks drawn back as if the birds were deeply affronted; the supersonic shape of the glossy ibis, their shot silk plumage turning now purple, now bronze, now green, as they wheeled back to their nests. In the deep water of this channel were long hair-like weeds, huge strands of them combed out by the gently moving current and, caught between the piles of twisted branches, resting on rafts of duckweed, each looking like sections of a beautiful mosaic floor made from tiny fragments of fine green jade. It was not only the sight but the sounds that were incredible. Apart from the noise of the cormorants there was the occasional harsh, deep, admonishing call of a heron; the tapping like a heartbeat of the woodpecker; the shrill babble of reed warblers; the purr and crackle of a passing dragonfly, like someone opening a special Christmas parcel; the swirl and clop of the catfish; the quarking of frogs in the reeds; the incessant cries of the myriad cuckoos like a convention of Swiss bankers chiming to each other; the sudden cackle of magpies like someone stirring up a winter fire; and over all the liquid sound of the water touching the boat as gently as a kitten drinking from a bowl of cream. It was a magical place and we were sorry to leave it, but we were now to travel beyond the Volga delta and on to the Kalmyk Autonomous Republic.

The object of this journey was to see and film what must be one of the strangest of cloven-hoofed mammals, the saiga. These are weird-looking creatures, about the size of a small goat, with lyre-shaped horns and a huge, bulbous nose, which they can whiffle about in the most extraordinary fashion. I had seen photographs of these creatures but never actually met one, so I was greatly looking forward to doing so. However, as it took us a journey of five hours on the river and seven hours over appalling roads to get to our

destination, my enthusiasm for meeting a saiga was on the wane. In incredible contrast to the almost overpoweringly lush delta we had come from, we were now in a kind of desiccated terrain called dry steppe, which merges here and there into semi-desert. It was flat land stretching to the horizon covered with low growth in green, silver and brown and, as it was spring, dotted with clusters of wild flowers. Towards evening we saw numerous graceful demoiselle cranes, delicate grey birds, many of which had young, and on one section of the road we saw a great concentration of steppe eagles, very handsome imperious-looking birds with a most graceful flight.

We drove on and on further and further into the steppe. During the seven-hour drive we passed only one village, which consisted of a handful of small houses, and the experience gave us once again a very vivid idea of the vastness of Russia. The sky was purple and green in which the sun was embedded like a fire opal and we were admiring this when we suddenly saw, silhouetted against it, a huge herd of saiga grazing placidly, their hooves kicking up little whirlwinds of dust as they moved. They had curiously heavy heads that looked almost too big for their bodies because of their ridiculous bulbous noses, but their horns were delicate and pale yellow like tallow. They were a magnificent sight as they moved slowly across the steppe with the coloured sky and the sinking sun as a backdrop, the young giving strange, harsh, rattling bleats to be answered in deeper tones by their mothers.

We drove on and I was just beginning to wonder if we were lost and our whitened bones would be found out on the steppe in a hundred years' time, when I saw a cluster of sparkling lights ahead. This was our camp site and what a camp site it proved to be. They had simply built for our convenience what could only be described as a mini-village in

Above and overleaf: The saiga is probably one of the most extraordinary of the steppe animals, with its huge nose, strange raucous, rattling bleat and its ringed horns, prized in the East as both medicine and aphrodisiac. It is also one of the great conservation stories, showing how, with care, we may live in harmony with the creatures that share this planet with us.

the middle of nowhere. There was a lavish kitchen, a huge tent for the crew to sleep in, two enormous *kabitkas* – one to act as a dining room and one to act as a bedroom-cum-living room for Lee and myself – separate showers and lavatories, and the whole thing included lights down our village 'street' lit by a gigantic generator. The fleet of transport that was lined up behind the kitchen consisted of our bus, two jeeps, three lorries, an ambulance and a biplane of considerable size. The organizer of this incredibly luxurious accommodation was the local television representative, an enchanting man who looked like

a reincarnation of Bhudda, and he was pleased at our obvious delight when he ushered us into our *kabitka*. A *kabitka* is a large, circular, dome-shaped construction like a lobster pot, covered with sheep wool felt. Inside, the floor and walls were covered with woven mats and blankets in gay colours, and on the floor there were mattresses and huge heaps of pillows and sheets. It was the most enchanting and comfortable of living quarters. Later, when we went to the *kabitka* dining room for a sumptuous meal, we found the walls lined with red silk hangings, which gave it a slightly oriental effect.

An 'instant' village (top) was erected for us by the local people in a remote part of the Kalmyk steppe, where we dined in a most unusual and elegant tent, called a kabitka (above).

The next day our private plane revved up and we went off saiga-spotting. We bumped off across the steppe, the plane wheels crushing the aromatic herbs, whose rich scent blew in through the door, left open so that Rodney could film through it. As we circled slowly over our little village our *kabitkas* looked extraordinarily like black mushroom tops pushing their way up through the green herbs of the steppes. In a comparatively short time we found a small herd of saiga, some thirty or forty animals, which panicked and ran ahead of us as we swooped down low to film, their biscuit-brown backs bobbing across the steppe, their small hooves kicking up tiny puffs of pale dust. Shortly after, we found bigger and bigger herds until the ground seemed to be a sea of saiga. It was a heart-warming sight, for early in this century the saiga herds had been so decimated by uncontrolled hunting that they were in danger of extinction. Then, in the nick of time, hunting was banned and gradually the saiga started to recover. From the few hundreds that were left the herds strengthened and multiplied and now there are over a million of them, with 170,000 in Kalmyk alone. This surely must be one of the most spectacular conservation stories.

We landed the plane near the herd and installed Rodney and Byron on the steppe and then, using the plane as a sort of sheep-or-saiga-dog, tried to drive the herd towards Rodney. The saigas, however, had other ideas and steadfastly refused to move in the direction we wanted

them to. After a number of frustrating attempts we had to give up since the young (although such sturdy little things that ten days after birth they can run at 50 miles an hour) were getting tired. So we flew back to our *kabitka* village and formulated another plan. This was that Rodney and Byron were dropped out in the steppe with a small tent, stayed the night there and hopefully at dawn the saiga herds would pass and they could film. Once again, however, the saigas were uncooperative. Finally, in desperation, we tried another method which, to our relief, worked. We installed the team as unobtrusively as possible (difficult in terrain as flat as a dining table) and with the jeeps gently chivvied the herd towards the camera. It took a lot of time and patience, but we finally got the results we wanted.

These steppes were wonderful and we were sorry to leave: sorry to leave our romantic and comfortable *kabitka*, sorry to leave the experience of getting up in a pearly blue dawn to make your way to the bathroom across a carpet of tiny thistles, a profusion of flowers in white and yellow and a mass of herbs that, as you crushed them underfoot, released their scents in the most miraculously redolent fashion. How wonderful for the saiga to live in this scented world, to eat and move on a carpet of aromas no chemist could reproduce in any test tube and to lie at night on a sweet-smelling bed of flowers.

In the kabitka where we worked and slept we were entertained with Kalmyk music and dancing by two girls in national costume. On the right is Professor Vladimir Flint, foremost Soviet ornithologist and our great friend, who has translated most of my books into Russian.

BUKHARA
Saving the saiga

БУХАРА

BUKHARA

We went to Bukhara to film the endangered goitred gazelle, such an ugly name for such a pretty animal.

FOR some horrendous reason, Russian planes leave at the most inconvenient hours. Our flight to Tashkent, for example, left Moscow at 1 a.m. and arrived at breakfast-time. Therefore we were feeling like a bouquet of flowers that had been sat on and partially devoured by an elephant. We lay about in our hotel room, trying to rid ourselves of this deleterious feeling until the plane was ready to take us on to Bukhara, a magical name for a place that I had long wanted to visit. We flew over a curious flat landscape of pale bronze- and coffee-coloured fields that looked like stiffly starched raw silk, patched here and there with fields of crops startling in their greenness, and then we swung over the jumbled city and could see, blurred by the heat haze, the brilliant blue domes of the mosques, like gigantic crocus buds pushing up through the rockery of houses. We were now in the heart of Uzbekistan.

If Moscow is a city of crows, then Bukhara is a city of turtledoves. They were everywhere, beautiful, sleek little birds with rich cinnamon-coloured backs. Incredibly tame, they were courting and mating under our very feet and the air rang with their demure liquid cooing – a most soothing and gentle noise. We went first to visit and film the various mosques for which Bukhara is famous. They really were dazzlingly splendid, ornamented with their mosaics of green and gold and blue, so that they looked as though they were draped in dragon's hide. The rather splendid tower called the Kalyan Minaret is shaped like an enormous brown pepper pot, 140 feet high. It is said that anyone who had offended the emir of the day was taken to the top and pushed off, to end in a very contrite bundle on the cobblestones below. Reputedly, the emir's favourite wife was once suspected of unfaithfulness and the emir (apparently a tetchy sort of man) condemned this wife to be cast off the tower to her death. The wife, however, indignant at being wrongly accused (or perhaps merely irritated that she had been found out) had other ideas as to what her fate should be. On the appointed day when she was to be cast from the tower top, she dressed with great care, putting on not only all her best jewellery but also as many skirts as she could. Thus, when she was given the final push and launched into space, the speed of her descent filled her skirts with air, ballooning them out into a sort of haute couture parachute, which carried her safely and gently to the ground. The emir, seeing this, decided that it was a sign that she had not been unfaithful and immediately forgave her, and so she lived happily in the harem ever after. It says a lot about the validity and trustworthiness of historical facts that I was told this same story about no less than three towers in three different cities in Central Asia.

The Kalyan mosque was very impressive. The huge courtyard, which can contain twelve thousand worshippers, is surrounded by beautifully decorated walls and arches. This mosque was undergoing renovations

Preceding page: We found many rare and delightful creatures in this strange desert country.

96

when we were there. Where parts of the vivid blue mosaic work were broken away, leaving a brown brick skeleton below, mynahs and tree sparrows had come to exploit the nooks and crannies thus revealed and had built in them nests like untidy wigs. Swifts were nesting under the arches and so squadrons of them were constantly zooming through the giant courtyard, giggling in the childish way that swifts do, sliding through and under the archways and doorways with a delicate precision that a Red Arrow pilot would envy.

In the centre of the great courtyard grew an enormous and ancient white mulberry tree, which was laden with fruit. Groups of girls and women had brought great plastic sheets, and while some of them held out the sheets, the more agile had swarmed into the branches and were

Bukhara is famous not only as a trading centre for fabulous carpets, but also for its blue-domed mosques, which seen through the heat haze as we flew in reminded me of huge crocus buds. We found the streets and buildings of the city alive with courting turtle doves, who made the air ring with their soft liquid cries.

The Kalyan minaret (above) from which, it is said, people who had offended the then emir were cast to their death. The storks' nest on top of the Kalyan dome (above right) is now empty and neglected, for the storks have left Bukhara forever. But the nest still provides shelter for sparrows and mynahs.

rocking to and fro, shaking the fat white fruits off in a shower. Eagerly they beckoned us across and insisted we devour handfuls of the luscious fruit, which, nothing loath, we did, before getting on with the serious business of filming.

On the dome, which looked like a monstrous blue cranium at one end of the courtyard, there was a stork's nest, an intricate jumble of twigs like some mad, upside-down Ascot hat. Alas, it was deserted and the tale of the storks who built it is a typical example of the way man interferes with and destroys nature. At one time, Bukhara was famous for two things – beautiful rugs and storks. The rugs, of course, were not made in Bukhara, but in other parts of the region, but they were brought to Bukhara to be sold. It was, in fact, the central marketplace and because of this, the richly decorated and beautiful floor and wall coverings became known as Bukhara rugs. Centuries ago, while everyone was busy weaving these exquisite rugs, the storks had discovered the mosques. They found the endless domes far superior to trees for the purposes of housebuilding and so persistent were they about this that the kindly Bukharans were forced to put a steel post in every dome so that when newly-wed storks started to build their nests, the laboriously collected twigs and branches did not simply slide off the blue, shiny surface of the dome like quicksilver off an egg. Thus it was that Bukhara became famous for its storks and each cerulean dome boasted its storks' nest. Storks are conservative birds and they build for the future, so each year they would return to their nests to reinforce and add to them, until the nests became as solid as the domes on which they were built. But after hundreds of years of this happy association came disaster in the form of what is called progress. For centuries the marshland and pools around Bukhara had provided the storks with rich bounty in the shape of frogs, fish, voles and water rats with which to feed themselves and their young. Now man, the stork's friend hitherto, cast envious eyes on these wetlands. It seems to be anathema to human beings to see a bog or swamp sparkling with

The massive Kalyan mosque has a huge mulberry tree in its courtyard where the local women were gathering the delicious fruits.

pools, alive with insects, birds and mammals and embroidered with flowers. They think that rich soil is being wasted, and that it is high time it was drained and the earth turned into agricultural land. This is precisely what happened at Bukhara. The lovely larder of the storks, the glittering acres where they could go and catch the amphibians and fish that abounded for feeding their young were drained and ploughed up and turned into regimented fields of crops. So the thousand-year friendship between Bukhara and the storks faltered and failed. Today, only a few of the indestructible nests (now a haven for sparrows, who build a nest within a nest) are left on the blue domes, but no storks, militarily upright in their black and white plumage, stand over them and clatter their scarlet bills like castanets. The blue domes of Bukhara are storkless and the city has lost something wonderful and precious. To be known as a city of rugs has, I suppose, a certain cachet about it, but to be known as a city of storks is surely infinitely more exotic.

One of the most spectacular of the archways in Bukhara is over the entrance to the Nadir Divan-bigi Madrasah, a school for Muslim religious teachers. It is decorated in a marvellous manner with a gigantic mosaic depicting a long-tailed bird carrying something in its feet. I had seen only photographs of this and had come to the conclusion it was a portrait of the mythological Phoenix, a bird that reputedly came from the area. However, when on close inspection it appeared to be carrying a deformed elephant in its talons, I revised my opinion and decided it must be Sinbad's famous Roc, which had a partiality for elephants. When I aired this opinion, the locals looked at

Drinking fine green tea in the gardens that flank the Nadir Divan-begi madrasah on which the beautiful mosaic of the simurg bird is depicted. It is carrying in its claws what local people say is a sheep and what looked to us like a misshapen and very unhappy elephant.

me in horror. This was no Roc, they said, but the Simurg bird, whose whole object in life was to help other animals. In this startling mural it was helping a sheep that had presumably lost its way. I said it did not *look* like a sheep and anyway from the expression on its face it was finding the attention of the Simurg bird acutely distasteful. It was smiling in gratitude, they assured me. After that I lost interest and contented myself with lying on an Uzbek tea bed in the sun and consuming some excellent green tea while admiring the mural but not worrying overmuch about its zoological significance. I could see that if I pursued my theory of a Roc with an elephant, it might provoke an ugly scene in the peaceful, flower-bedecked garden.

Our chief reason for visiting Bukhara was, of course, to see the nearby desert breeding centre in which lives the goitred gazelle as well as a herd of kulan. The saving of this gazelle is an interesting story. The wild population was almost completely eradicated and it was obvious that something drastic would have to be done if the animal was to be saved. A large number of gazelles had been kept as pets and a plan was worked out to try to obtain these specimens. First, a large area of some desert with black saxual groves (a curious twisted tree with leaves like segmented pine needles) was set aside and fenced for security. Then a campaign was launched in the press and on television explaining the plight of the gazelle and asking people if they would donate their pets to the new breeding centre. Once the urgency of the matter had been explained, people rallied round and in a short time fifty pet gazelles had been gathered together. This was some years ago and now their numbers have risen to hundreds. So successful, indeed, has this centre

been that gazelles are now exported to stock other breeding centres in the Soviet Union and will eventually be used to re-stock their former range.

The centre's headquarters was a cluster of small houses by a tiny lake, its reed-fringed shores alive with birds – kingfishers, stilts, reed warblers and beautiful bluethroats, elegant, colourful, tail-wagging little birds. We first visited the tame gazelles and the young ones that the staff were in the process of hand-rearing. The youngsters were charming little creatures with coats the colour of butterscotch, huge brilliant dark eyes, and large ears like fur-covered arum lilies. They were completely fearless and either sat in our laps sucking our fingers or else wobbled around us on their long, lanky legs.

Near the pens in which these gazelles were kept, we found a group of very tame susliks. These small, squirrel-like rodents are rotund in shape with huge bulbous eyes and short tails. Their backs are a rich, reddish-brown and their shirt-fronts an immaculate cream colour. They live in colonies in subterranean 'cities' that they excavate, and they are found in such quantities that they form an important food source for all the desert predators. This colony was very busy about its business, digging new burrows in a flurry of sandy soil, eating, running from one burrow to another on mysterious errands and stopping periodically to stand up, straight as guardsmen, their paws dangling down their shirt-fronts, watching our activities with their prominent shining eyes, their whiskers quivering with interest.

When we had finished filming the susliks, we drove out into the desert in pursuit of the wild gazelles and the kulan. The desert was flat,

The black saxaul tree is most important in the desert, acting not only as a windbreak but also, with its strong root system, keeping the shifting sands at bay.

These enchanting baby gazelles, only a few weeks old, were being hand reared. There are plans to send them to another desert reserve to found a new herd.

At this stage in their careers baby gazelles are very vulnerable, being innocent, trusting and still very wobbly on their elegant long legs. Their only defence is their coloration; when their mothers go off to graze, the babies stay curled on the ground, invisible against the pale desert shrubs and sand.

Overleaf: Down at the tiny reed-fringed lake there was a great assembly of birds, including (from the top) the handsome black-headed form of the yellow wagtail dancing about, pecking at the myriad insects; the stilts, walking through the shallows on their long, slender legs; and the male and female bluethroats – the first I had ever seen. Towards sunset, the reed beds rang with the songs of these and other birds.

Ground squirrel colonies form large and busy 'townships' of many animals. They are quick, inquisitive little rodents of great charm, though the farmers claim that their complex underground dwellings damage the soil. However, as they were there before the farmers, I think they should be left in peace.

fawn-coloured sand, as fine as talcum powder, dotted with saxual bushes and starred with tiny multicoloured desert flowers. Some were like pyramids of pale lavender trumpets, some like little white balls with furry, bright orange centres, so they looked like poached eggs and others had domino-shaped petals of bright yellow spotted with a rich deep orange. They were quite lovely and looked very gay in this desiccated and waterless terrain. The trees were full of turtledoves and handsome tree sparrows and at one point we saw a hoopoe, breast pink as a salmon, dancing along the sand with his Red Indian war bonnet erect, searching for beetles among the saxual trees. These trees were mainly about six to nine feet tall, though there were some venerable clumps that were older and taller. The saxual is a strange tree, with an ability to flourish in the most arid and inhospitable of terrains. Owing to its survival capacity and the fact that it acts as both windbreak and sandbinder, a grove of saxual six miles wide and 125 miles long has been planted round Bukhara to prevent the desert from encroaching and swallowing up this city of blue mosques.

We drove for some considerable distance across this curious bleached desert before we found the wild gazelles, a small group of about twenty, their horns shining like tar in the sun as they meandered through a grove of baby saxuals. They were very wary, but by careful driving we managed to get comparatively close to them. We watched and filmed them for some time and then suddenly, for no apparent reason, they panicked and ran off through the miniature saxual forest, appearing and disappearing as they bounded like pale fawn fish leaping in a green river. We drove after them, hoping that they might stop, but their panic was too great and they put on an amazing burst of speed and were soon lost in the shimmering heat haze that made the horizon tremble like melting glass.

We drove back to the headquarters for lunch and then examined all the desert creatures that had been amassed for us to film. This star-studded cast included a huge, chocolate-coloured tarantula,

Even in this harsh desert country you could find a wealth of flowers that showed up like jewels against the dry monochromatic backgrounds.

furry as a kitten, a scorpion as long as a teaspoon, which looked as though it had been carved out of ancient, yellowing ivory, and some fine fat geckos with charcoal-grey skins marked with gay canary-yellow spots and yellowish faces in which huge glittering eyes were embedded like jewels. What made these reptiles so enchanting was that their mouths curved up at the corners in a shy smile and each had a black line over its huge eyes that ridiculously made them look as though they were wearing very long and very thick false eyelashes. There was also an appealing desert hedgehog, with long legs, a boot-button nose and long ears like a donkey. But undoubtedly the star of the show was a four-foot-long desert monitor that had been obtained for us, who sat fuming with rage in a long wire cage. He had a brick-red skin with a handsome series of spots and stripes that made him look as though he was wearing a black lace shawl of very modern design. If you approached his cage, he put on a fine display of arrogant anger. He would stand up, stiff-legged, back arched, his throat puffed out, hissing like a kettle on coals, and through his open mouth his yellow tongue would flail the air while he lashed the bars of the cage with his whip-like tail, a tail that could slice you like a bullwhip or blind you if it slashed across your face.

We drove all these stars out into the desert, released each one into an appropriate setting and filmed them. They were all most cooperative, the tarantula giving a good display of ferocity, the scorpion curving its tail like a pale amber jug handle, the hedgehog trotting about with its ears pricked, and the geckos wandering about with their thick eyelashes, their ingenuous eyes and their demurely smiling mouths like beautiful little schoolgirls wearing their first make-up. Then we came to the monitor.

He had been sitting in his cage, glowering at us and hissing faintly, his tail curved at the ready. Now our job was to get him out of the cage, with no damage to either him or us and release him into a suitable setting. I pointed out to John Hartley that under 'occupation' in his

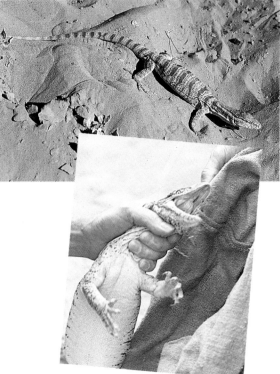

The desert monitor (above right). Here he is about to engulf John Hartley's thumb (right). Shortly afterwards, he was released and stalked, hissing angrily to himself, across his parched kingdom. The elusive and handsome kulan (above), a small herd of which shares the reserve with the gazelles.

Opposite insets: *The charming desert hedgehog with ears like a donkey, and the velvety-skinned geckoes, one who looked as if it were wearing false eyelashes.*

passport, he had been silly enough to enter the magic word 'herpetologist', so the job of getting the monitor to act should by rights fall to him. Nothing loath, John armed himself with a large sack and set about the task. He opened the cage and stuffed the sack inside in an endeavour to wrap the monitor's head in it. However, the reptile, with lightning speed, grabbed a large mouthful of the sack in a vice-like grip. Having got the biting bit of the monitor occupied, so to speak, John could reach in, grab him by the back of his neck and his lengthy tail and haul him out. This he did, but then we were faced with a problem. The monitor flatly refused to let go of the sack. As we did not think that film of a monitor walking about in the desert with a large sack in its mouth would look even remotely natural, we had to find some way to get him to relinquish his booty. Prising his mouth open was unthinkable, for we would risk breaking his jaw bones, so fierce was his grip. We finally decided that as he had only a comparatively small portion of the sack in his mouth we would cut the rest of it off very close to his lips and then the offending sack inside his mouth would not be visible. Just as John had completed a very neat job of cutting the sack free, the monitor opened his mouth wide, spat out the piece of sack and closed his mouth again with a snap with John's thumb inside. Eventually, we managed to extract John's thumb from the monitor's jaw, but not before his thumbnail had been split and the side of his thumb nastily mangled. Then we carried the monitor out to a piece of desert that was not bespattered with John's life-blood and released him. I must say that in spite of all the trouble he had caused us, he behaved very well, stalking through his desert kingdom, hissing thoughtfully to himself, pausing now and then to survey the saxual groves with a gleaming eye and finally disappearing down a suslik hole, which I am glad to be able to report was unoccupied.

The only thing we had left to film now were the kulan and these were not easy to track down. We drove round for some considerable time before we actually found them. They were standing out in a rather arid patch of desert with scarcely any saxual bushes around. A herd of some twelve animals, the mares and foals were bunched together, while the dominant stallion remained on guard some two hundred yards away. His wives and young obviously looked to him to give them the right signals for although they were alarmed at our presence, all they would do was mill around in a tight circle or else run a few yards and then return to their former position, while the stallion remained impassive, head up, eyeing us imperiously. They were fine, sleek, mule-like animals, their fawn-coloured hides gleaming in the setting sun, their dark manes as crisp as newly clipped hedges. Eventually they seemed to lose some of their fear of us and they settled down, so we managed to get some nice footage of them. But after about a quarter of an hour, for no apparent reason (perhaps we were becoming too bold) the stallion decided that enough was enough and he gave some imperceptible signal for his harem and young to move. They wheeled round almost as one animal, the stallion bringing up the rear, then they galloped off deeper into the desert, their dark hooves churning up the sand, so that they seemed to be dragging a great cumulus cloud of white behind them.

CHATKAL
From Tien Shan to Samarkand

ЧАТКАЛ
CHATKAL

The fabled city of Samarkand, smouldering in the heat haze. How we wished we could have entered it on camels instead of an Aeroflot flight.

Opposite: *Samarkand is a city of huge domes and massive archways, many undergoing the most complex restoration work. One of the most impressive architectural achievements is the gigantic arch of Shir Dar madrasah (inset), flamboyantly decorated with fierce tigers and blazing suns.*

Preceding page: *The snow-covered hills of Chatkal, and (inset) the market in Samarkand.*

WE were to fly from Bukhara to Samarkand. The plane was late, but on this occasion we did not mind, as Bukhara airport is very pleasant and we could doze in the shade on benches set under gnarled and ancient apple trees. At last we took off and as we flew over the flat landscape, I could not help feeling it was rather *infra dig* to enter such a fabled city by such modern and conventional means of transport. Alexander the Great probably came to it on horseback as did Genghis Khan, but Marco Polo, being a romantic Italian, must surely have entered it on a great, flat-footed, woolly, two-humped Bactrian camel, whereas the best we could do was to arrive in a smelly, noisy plane. Progress has certainly taken a lot of the romance out of travel.

We descended towards Samarkand and in the heat haze we could see the blue domes of the mosques like the eggs in some fabulous bird's nest. The drive into this ancient city must surely be one of the nicest and most exotic in the world. As well as massive domes, glossy as jewels, we passed gigantic archways picked out in mosaics, all of sea-green, yellow and lapis lazuli tiles. The wide, tree-lined streets were thronged with people in a bewildering variety of brilliant national costumes, a sort of living Persian rug. Set into the walls running along the boulevards were tiny shops, some with a frontage of only ten feet, but with wide counters on which were piled legs of lamb, chickens, silk shawls like baby rainbows, bales of multi-coloured cloth and foodstuffs of every description. There was an Arabian Nights quality about the whole scene that was most exhilarating.

Having settled in, we spent the afternoon touring the mosques and the market with a charming guide called Inez, searching for suitable film locations. Inez spoke impeccable English and was very knowledgeable. The courtyards round the mosques were impressive and the coloured tile work intricate and beautiful. Many were in the process of restoration, a huge and complex task, for in many cases the foundation had shifted over the centuries, sending cracks skittering up to the domes and arches like cracks in thawing ice. The first problem was to devise a way of reinforcing the base of these mammoth structures with concrete. It was some time before a way to do this was worked out, but once it had been perfected, the task of restoration could start. All the cracked tiles had to be removed and replaced by ones made by the same method and with the same colours. The bricks to which the tiles were originally attached had to be faced with cement as well, to give a firmer surface for the tiles to adhere to. This is an enormous undertaking that will take many years to complete, but eventually this facelift should enable the mosques and their complex arches, which have lasted thousands of years, to grace the world with their beauty for ever.

The insides of the buildings look as intricately beautiful as the outsides, and are filled with such a rich selection of humanity that you are not sure whether you should study architecture or ethnology.

The market was magnificent and so colourful and lovely that one was bedazzled. All the young women looked Tibetan, with peach-bloom complexions and fine, dark almond-shaped eyes. Many of them wore their hair in long, thick plaits and the newlyweds wore beautifully decorated little round hats. The standard costume seemed to be a brightly coloured dress that ended at the knees and below this silk trousers, some most elaborately embroidered with gold thread and sequins. All the old ladies were massive, with breasts and buttocks like watermelons and splended brown faces covered with a spider's web of wrinkles. The old men, lean and brown as biltong, had hawk-beak noses and grey beards like Spanish moss. They wore huge leather boots and carefully wound turbans or else small round black hats embroidered in silver.

The produce for sale was prodigious. Banks of carrots and cabbages, tottering pyramids of yellow apples, mounds of spices in a hundred different colours, piles of blonde raisins like wrinkled amber beads, baskets of roasted and salted apricot seeds, agape from the heat of the fire, looking like a mass of goose barnacles.

In a huge building was the milk and money market, a memorable spectacle. There were giant jugs of cream and milk and amongst them, perched precariously on sheets of plastic, piles of fresh curds, presided over by fat ancient great-grandmothers, wrinkled as lizards, shrill as parakeets, their brown hands bespattered with curds as they tried to keep the tottering heaps from sliding off the plastic sheets on to the floor. Further along was the butter in enormous bricks, some pale daffodil-yellow, others shining like gold nuggets. Part of the

The entrance to the fantastic market, which was old in the time of Marco Polo and where he no doubt did his shopping. In the background you can see the restoration work in progress on this huge mosque of Bibi-Khanum.

building was devoted to honey and here again the colours were extraordinary. Honey as pale yellow as a buttercup, honey as brown as a bear, honey so dark it looked like tar, all of it gleaming and with the rich, heavy musky scent that honey has, an amalgam of a thousand flowers. On parts of the counters, honeycombs had been stacked haphazardly in large tin bowls and then liquid honey poured over them so that they looked like exotic reefs in amber seas.

In a market as huge and vibrant as this, you soon get bewildered and end up with only a series of tiny vignettes in your mind: men, fierce-looking, with huge daggers in their belts, standing by a blue painted stall and drinking great tankards of beer, each with a head of froth like a summer cloud; a shady corner where cockerels, chickens, ducks and turkeys lay, legs tied together in cacophonous feathered bundles: a dark, arched alleyway, leading out to a sun-drenched courtyard, and as I glanced down it, a three-foot-high dwarf, as if on a brightly lit stage, swaggered through, almost dancing, a chicken in one hand and an apple in the other. There were sprouting potatoes, scaly-skinned, with pale green pink-tipped fingers thrusting up, surrounded by groups of people, frowning earnestly, examining them with all the care of an art critic summing up a Rembrandt. There was an old, old man, with a face like a newly born rhesus monkey, all wrinkles, sunken cheeks and worried eyes. He was wearing a small turban and an astonishingly long blue coat, the sleeves of which dangled nine inches beyond his hands. Bent as a croquet hoop, he ambled from place to place with tortoise-like slowness and determination, pausing frequently to sit down in the sun and doze for a minute or two. The floors of the entire market were as speckled as a thrush's egg with spittle and I felt that after walking fifty feet the soles of my shoes would have

Below and opposite: A magnificent market of everything for everybody. Rainbows of vegetables and fruit, huge white cumulus clouds of curds, and every conceivable colour of honey, rich and musky. The market, starting at dawn, was at its height at mid-morning. Again there was such a wonderful variety of people that we had difficulty in concentrating on the exotic produce they were buying and selling, from green tea to homemade snuff to roasted apricot seeds.

accumulated such an assortment of germs that Louis Pasteur would have been enchanted to have received them as a present. It was one of the most lively and wonderful markets that I have ever been in and one would have to spend a couple of weeks in it to do it justice. When you think that it was old in the time of Genghis Khan and that Marco Polo probably did his shopping in it, it gives you an extraordinary feeling of the past being in the present.

We flew from Samarkand back to Tashkent where we learnt, to my irritation, that the road to our next destination – the Chatkal Reserve on the edge of the Tien-Shan Mountains – had been destroyed by a landslide. To get to it would necessitate a four-hour jeep ride and then six hours on horseback. The team decided to undertake this somewhat hazardous adventure in the hopes of getting good film, while Lee and I would fly into the reserve by helicopter.

The beginning of the Chatkal range in the Tien-Shan Mountains still ribbed with last winter's snow. The flight in by helicopter was breathtakingly beautiful as the sun caught these snow clefts, turning them now white, now blue and then pink.

In certain places the snow was churned up as if by the boots of a giant. These were the graveyards of the winter avalanches that crumpled off the hillsides and roared and boomed into the valleys, sometimes carrying huge boulders and trees with them in a spectacular display of strength.

It was a wonderful flight. At first we flew over flat, toffee-coloured terrain with here and there orchards or patches of alfalfa, with an occasional glittering skein of river. Then we struck the foothills of the Tien-Shan Mountains and the scenery was unbelievably beautiful. In every direction the knife-edged hills coiled like snakes, green and yellow, their flanks striped with snow and here and there outcrops of rust-red rocks, embedded in the snow like shelled walnuts in sugar. Gradually we dropped lower and lower, chasing our own shadow as it whisked over the snowfields, until we were flying down valleys with the mountains towering above us, where the rock faces were fox-red and the lower slopes shaggy with pine forests interspersed with wild apple trees heavy with blossom and great sheets of yellow flowers that looked like mustard fields. Finally we landed in a tiny valley that was ablaze with colour. The slopes were covered with the yellow flowers we had seen from the air, which turned out to be a plant resembling fennel. Amongst it grew wild rhubarb, with dark green, plate-shaped leaves and rose-pink stems, banks of red and yellow tulips, their petals looking newly varnished, and throughout the valley groves of apple in a froth of pink and white blossom. The sun was brilliantly warm, the sky as blue as a hedge sparrow's egg and the air cool and fresh. We decided that this was the most beautiful place we had so far visited in the Soviet Union.

As the sound of our noisy arrival faded away into tiny echoes in the valley, there appeared from the apple trees the reserve director and a band of his helpers. The director was a fine-looking elderly man with a kindly, wrinkled face and humorous eyes. His helpers were a cheerful group of unkempt ruffians with dark Mongolian faces and glittering black eyes. White and gold teeth flashed in equal quantities in their

Our final destination was a flower-
filled valley, pink and white with
apple blossom on which electric
blue carpenter bees fed, with banks
of wild fennel and pink-stalked
rhubarb and everywhere a blaze of
scarlet tulips. No less than 1400
species of plants have been found in
the Chatkal Reserve, many of them
very rare.

Top: *It is said that this lovely tulip from Chatkal – now endangered – is the one from which all our domestic tulips were derived.*

Above: *The handsome little red-fronted serin in tiny flocks searched for insects in the apple blossom.*

brown faces as they shouldered our bags and equipment and strode off through the wild apple orchards, with toast-brown fritillaries, black admirals and bronze dragonflies wheeling about their legs as they threaded their way through the tulips and fennel.

Our accommodation was a tiny house nestling in apple trees on the banks of a small busy river, icy-cold, clear as glass, sliding down over its bed of amber-coloured rocks in a great series of silver ringlets. Its endless chatter day and night was as soothing as a beehive.

As we had been told that no food was to be had up on the reserve, we had dutifully visited the market in Tashkent and brought up a massive supply of vegetables, fruit, rice and bones for making stock. So, as soon as we had partaken of breakfast with the director – a breakfast that in his case was a liquid one consisting of Georgian brandy served neat – I got some of our wild-looking but good-natured friends to light a large fire. I filled a large cauldron full of water and marrow bones and let it simmer for a couple of hours and then added the vegetables we had brought and the rice. The result was a thick and delicious soup, which was just what we needed up there for, though the sun was hot, if you sat in the shade you were soon shivering. After lunch, the director – who by now had had enough brandy and had made inroads into a large jerry can of local Uzbek wine – was helped off to bed by one of his minions to take a well-earned nap. Lee and I went for a walk down the valley, along the banks of the stream. There was nothing but the murmur of water and bird-song and the cool, clear air was filled with the scent of apple blossom. It was strange to see that the conglomeration of insects included old friends, like Apollo and

Top: *A valley so filled with sweet-scented flowers naturally attracted many butterflies and among the most spectacular were the southern swallowtail in its handsome livery of yellow and black (left), and the Apollo spotted like a leopard (right).*

Above: *The huge griffon vulture we were lucky enough to film had built its nest in the top of a pine tree, an unusual choice of site for griffon vultures.*

Left: *The vultures feed on the carcases of large mammals, and now are found only where wild goats and sheep still roam.*

Menzbieri's marmot is a charming and rare rodent that lives in small colonies high in the Chatkal range. Its alarm call – a piercing whistle – can be heard echoing round the cliffs when it sees danger approaching. During the winters it hibernates deep in underground galleries while the fierce blizzards rage outside, making life above ground impossible.

swallowtail butterflies and carpenter bees, as well as flies and beetles I had never seen before. The great piles of blossom had attracted hosts of bee flies – russet-red, furry as teddy bears, with glittering wings. Their flying abilities were prodigious, for they could hover stationary, and then with incredible speed zoom off in any direction, even backwards. Anyone who thinks human beings have solved all the problems of aerodynamics should watch a bee fly at work. The trees were full of birds – woodpeckers tapping away like carpenters, jays flashing blue and pink as they flew, shrikes, tree sparrows and a flock of red-fronted serins, the first I had ever seen.

As evening drew on and the shadows slid into the valley, muting the flower colours, it became very chilly and we piled on all the clothing we possessed and huddled round the fire, glad of the warmth we could extract from the director's stock of Georgian brandy. While he had been sleeping, his band of merry men had been up the valley and returned with their hats full of field mushrooms, each as big as a doll's parasol, fleshy and fragrant. These were added to the *pilov* they were constructing in an enormous battered frying pan. When it was served it proved to be delicious, and when we were stuffed to capacity we tumbled into our sheepskin sleeping bags. At about half past one in the morning we were rudely awoken by an incredible rumpus, people laughing and shouting, the neighing of horses, the jangle of stirrups and bits. It sounded as if we were being relieved by the US cavalry, but it turned out to be the team, saddle-sore and frozen stiff, but in great good spirits, as they had not only seen and filmed (the terms are not synonymous) a griffon vulture on its nest and several Siberian ibex but, of all fortunate things, they had got good footage of a colony of Menzbieri's marmots, one of the Soviet Union's endangered species.

Marmots are a widespread group of large fat rodents and different species occur from the Alps in Europe through the Soviet Union into China, and from Alaska down into the northern half of the United States. The Menzbieri's marmot is found only in a small area of the Tien-Shan Mountains, where it was once common. However, agricul-

tural encroachment of the low mountainous valleys has driven it back further and further into the mountains and it is thought that this remnant population numbers only a few thousand animals. Marmots are robust, stocky creatures with thick stumpy tails. The type the team had filmed was dark brown on the back, fading to rusty-red on the tail and with an elegant cream-coloured shirt-front and forelegs. The Menzbieri's marmots are communal, digging long and complex burrows, where they give birth to their young, and which they use for the important process of hibernation, which in some of the more brutal parts of their range may be for nine months of the year. They are very keen-sighted and sit upright at the mouths of their burrows scanning the scenery for danger. Anything remotely suspicious and their warning call, a loud and piercing whistle, can be heard echoing round the cliffs of their mountain. Fat-faced and cuddly-looking, the marmot is a charming rodent and to have got film of such a rare creature in such difficult terrain was incredible luck.

We spent one more day filming in this enchanting flower-filled valley and bade our host and his helpers a fond goodbye. As the chopper rose, the rush of wind from our propellers blew hundreds of apple blossoms from the trees in a great pink and white cloud, and bent the glossy yellow and blood-red heads of the tulips, so they looked as if they were bowing a farewell to us.

The Siberian ibex is a handsome member of the goat family and lives high in the mountains in the most difficult of terrain, where it hears only bird song and the roar and swish of avalanches. Sure-footed and keen-eyed, it is extremely difficult to approach in its mountain fastness.

REPETEK
Red desert

PEПETEK

REPETEK

Camels are extremely useful in the desert, as we found out, but nevertheless it is difficult to work up a real love for a creature with such a sour and lugubrious expression.

THE centre of Chardzhou, in eastern Turkmenistan, was pleasant with neat, colourful wooden houses and well-kept gardens, but as we got to the suburbs the houses became more ramshackle and the gardens had broken fences and piles of rusting machinery, empty tins and bottles and the general seedy air of a gypsy encampment. But very soon we left the town behind and the road meandered out into the desert on the way to the Repetek Reserve. It was rolling scrub desert with silver-green shrubs, many of them covered with yellow and pink balls of blossom. These blossoms when seen close-to are very curious, for they resemble – of all things – a sort of vegetable sea anemone, as they consist of a round ball of yellow or pink fluff from which spring the tentacles of petals, like froth, forming a semi-transparent ball. Along the telegraph wires that lined the road sat dozens of bee-eaters and rollers, brilliant as jewels in the bright sunshine. Here and there among the lion-tawny sandhills stood small groups of dyspeptic-looking dromedaries, their mouths full of flowers that they chomped on stolidly.

The reserve headquarters were immensely impressive. Our accommodation had such unexpected luxuries as air conditioning, electric lights, fans, comfortable beds and even a refrigerator. There was an elegant dining hall and washroom and shower facilities, all set in gardens of flowering shrubs and trees. The director was a handsome, dark-skinned man who looked Indonesian. He was solemn at first but soon displayed a mischievous sense of humour when he realized that we did not take ourselves too seriously.

What we wanted to show on film was the desert generally, but in particular the desert tortoise and the desert sparrow, a bird once thought to be extinct until it was discovered, alive and well and living in Repetek. Also, knowing that to try to find the local reptiles with our limited time schedule was going to be difficult, we had arranged for Moscow Zoo to ship down a representative collection of reptiles for us to film *in situ*. So we had our preliminary meeting with the director and he immediately filled us with gloom and despondency. First, the Moscow Zoo people could not get a flight. Second, the brief and frenzied sex life of the tortoise had come to an end, and they had all buried themselves in the sand to aestivate during the wickedly brilliant summer sunshine. As we talked it was already 114°F in the shade in the late spring, so we could sympathize with them. Then we came to the desert sparrow. This, he said, was seldom seen and so our chances of filming it were, in his opinion, nil. Having thus crushed all our hopes, he poured out vodka, which by that time we were in urgent need of since we could see our chances of filming a desert show vanishing. Seeing our distress, the director tried to soothe us by saying that after

Preceding page: The desert and (inset) trees that looked dead but could burst into bloom at the slightest rainfall.

128

These extraordinary and beautiful bushes are called locally 'A Thousand Suns'. To me they looked like very elegant whipped ice cream. Not only did they add great beauty to the arid landscape but also provided a source of food for numerous insects.

Even with the blistering temperatures you could still find small bouquets of greenery in the most unlikely places.

lunch – when the heat had died down somewhat – we could go out into the desert so we could get some idea of what there was to film. This plan we agreed to and after an excellent lunch, followed by a siesta, we set off. We decided that Lee and I would go one way and the crew would go another, thus allowing us to cover more ground. We set off in a mammoth truck with gigantic tyres designed to carry the vehicle over the rolling dunes of fine, shifting sand, called barkhans, so typical of the Karakum Desert. These extraordinary vast mountains of sand move during the different seasons like the sea, for at one time of the year the wind pushes them one way and then, as the seasons change, the wind veers round and pushes the dunes back to their original position. You could say that these immense waves of sand undergo a tidal movement similar to an ocean. The sand was basically the colour of a pale camel-hair coat with a pinkish tinge in the shadows and a silvery cast in the sun. We chugged and roared up and down these fifty- to sixty-foot-high dunes and it was like being on a huge sandy roller coaster. Once we had passed the barkhans, which were fairly arid and lifeless, we entered the zone where there was more vegetation – various grasses, black saxual groves and a curious tree like a weeping willow that looked very out of place in such a waterless and dry terrain. There was an extraordinary amount of life here in what, after all, one would have thought to be a pretty lifeless part of our planet. Apart from the trees there were many desert flowers, the predominant one looking like a lavender column of miniature larkspurs, and others like minute buttercups freckled with red. There were dozens of birds to be heard but not seen in the saxual groves, for the heat was still stunning, and so

they lurked in the shadows. The insects and arachnids seemed impervious to the heat, however, and spiders of several species abounded, as well as the flat black ticks, like little circular coins with legs, who dashed busily about on the burning sand. Everywhere there were beetles — torpedo-shaped ones, two inches long, green as emeralds dusted with gold, others, black as a witch's hat, boldly spotted with circular white spots, and dung beetles as big as matchboxes glowing blue-black in the sun as they flew ponderously about in search of the wherewithal to fashion their nurseries. Stalking the dunes were net-backed lizards, beautiful reptiles, a rich grass—green, with a black patterning that made them look as though they were wearing black lace shawls. They moved in rapid little rushes, skittering from place to place, pausing now and again to sniff at the sand and then dig down into it in their search for insects. Certainly the commonest reptiles and the most extraordinary ones were the two species of toad-headed lizards that were everywhere, and so bold they would let you approach to within a couple of feet of them. Their round blunt heads and their bodies were covered with pointed scales like minute pyramids, and the toes on their large feet were fringed so they acted like snowshoes as they moved over the fine sand. They had some amusing habits that were most endearing. Whenever they stopped in their incessant hunt for food they stood on their heels, their toes held up in the air. It appeared to be a method of sitting on the burning sand without getting your toes burnt, but was the heel impervious to heat? It was a most curious habit and I must say they looked very funny sitting on their heels while their long fringed toes waved about gently,

Most people imagine a desert is lifeless but this is far from the case. Here you find clumps of small bushes that when dead wander in the wind like tumble weeds (top).

Here and there are little bright clumps of flowers like tiny trumpets. Then, of all unexpected things, you find a toadstool sticking up from the sand, and everywhere there are beetles, some of which have been preyed on by birds and their wing cases dropped like exotic jewels.

like a concert pianist flexing his fingers before embarking on a complex piece of Chopin. Their other habits were even more extraordinary. One of the species, if you approached too closely, would warn you of its displeasure by unfolding a blood red flange of skin at the corners of its open mouth. The other species would suddenly curl its tail up like a watch spring, showing the underside which, in contrast to the somewhat drab cinnamon coloration of the rest of its body, was startlingly white striped with black. The effect of these unexpected displays on potential predators can be imagined.

We found our first venture into the desert fascinating and,

The desert lizards were charming. The sand toad-headed lizard (below left and bottom) has the habit of sitting on its heels and flexing its fingers as if about to play a piano concerto, or curling up its tail like a watch spring, and the eared toad-headed lizard (below right) frightens you by opening two scarlet flanges on each side of its mouth, but infinitely prefers to be left alone.

although the heat was intense, it was so dry that you did not really notice it. As the evening approached, we roller-coasted back over the teddy-bear-brown dunes, now with each wind ripple picked out in blue, and a fox, red as an autumn leaf, and two hares fled at our noisy approach. We were just admiring the setting sun, like a giant marigold sinking into a powder-blue sky, when Lee gave a frantic squeal and shouted to the driver to stop. She leapt out and raced back down the road to reappear shortly, out of breath and triumphant, carrying a desert tortoise, who was looking most indignant about the whole thing and, to show his annoyance, proceeded to copiously irrigate both us and the interior of the vehicle. But we did not mind, for we had found at least one of the creatures we had come so far to meet. When we got back to the reserve headquarters another piece of good news awaited us. The director and our crew had hardly entered the desert when the director spotted a desert sparrow's nest. Rodney set up a camera and got shots of both the cock and the hen birds bringing nesting material to complete their home. It was a real triumph to have got film of this, one of the rarest of all Soviet birds. In addition we were delighted to find that Vladimir Frulov, the Moscow Zoo curator of reptiles, had, by bribery, bluff and bluster, forced his way on to the plane from Moscow, determined that we should not be let down. A handsome young man, he had brought with him a rucksack that contained a spare shirt, three sand boas and a cobra, which any true herpetologist would consider to be a very sensible choice of items to have in your luggage. We went to bed in high spirits, which made a change, for generally at the end of a hard day's work you tended to run down your achievements.

The next day we were up and away by six to avoid the blistering

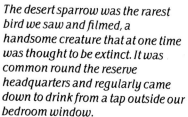

The desert sparrow was the rarest bird we saw and filmed, a handsome creature that at one time was thought to be extinct. It was common round the reserve headquarters and regularly came down to drink from a tap outside our bedroom window.

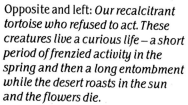

Opposite and left: Our recalcitrant tortoise who refused to act. These creatures live a curious life – a short period of frenzied activity in the spring and then a long entombment while the desert roasts in the sun and the flowers die.

morning sun later on. It was a beautiful morning with a brilliant blue sky, even at that hour blurred with heat haze. In this morning light the barkhans looked tawny-bronze and the wind ripples showed up marvellously so that each dune looked like the desiccated hide and rib cage of some enormous long-dead dinosaur. In this brittle morning sunlight the strange round globe-like flowers on the bushes looked exactly like tiny helpings of strawberry and lemon ice cream served among the branches. We had taken our precious tortoise with us and he behaved like the worst sort of temperamental old-time Hollywood film star. Either he just sat in his shell and sulked, or else, if we wanted him to walk from left to right, he stubbornly refused to do anything but walk from right to left. When we had rearranged the whole script so that he *could* walk from right to left, he steadfastly walked from left to right.

These desert tortoises – in spite of being such reluctant film stars – are handsome beasts, with a nicely marked shell in pale brown and chocolate, and with enormously long and very-well-manicured-looking nails on their toes. They have adapted themselves to live a very precarious life in the desert, for they are entirely dependent on the ephemeral spring flowers and grasses, which have a short life of two to three months before the heat of the summer devours them. Therefore the tortoise has a scant three months in which to feed itself and form a layer of fat on which it can exist during its long aestivation, and during this short period it must mate and lay eggs as well. So the short spring months are a busy time for it as it trundles across the desert feeding on

The sand boas (below) were charming, gentle snakes but they (like most of our reptile stars) refused to cooperate and do the things we wanted them to do. However, the Central Asian cobra (opposite), maybe because he was born in Moscow, was very proud and did everything we asked of him in an impeccable manner.

tiny flowers, digging nests for its eggs, and finally choosing a suitable spot to bury itself for its long sleep while the summer sun bakes the desert like a cake.

After we had finally got the reluctant tortoise to give a passable performance, we turned our attention to the sand boas. These were handsome little beasts some twelve inches long with a pale fawn skin nicely marked with brownish blotches. Their heads were tiny, flattened and spade-shaped, presumably because this makes it easier for them to burrow in the sand in which they live. Naturally their subterranean behaviour was what we wanted to show. After all, if you show a snake that lives *in* sand you want to show it burrowing into the sand. The boas had other ideas. They dashed off at top speed on the surface of the sand, they coiled themselves round bushes, they sat immobile as if stuffed. In short, they did everything except burrow. At the end of a frustrating hour we finally got one to bury himself, but with the utmost reluctance as though it were a thing that no well-bred sand boa normally did, but he would do, just this once, to oblige us.

After our difficulties with the tortoise and the sand boas, I viewed our encounter with the cobra with some trepidation, but to our delight he behaved beautifully, hamming it up like an old professional film star. He spread his hood and waved to and fro, he hissed, he coiled and uncoiled, he wriggled through bushes with obviously malevolent intent, he peered from behind fallen logs with a beady eye, and although he did not twist his moustaches like a villain in an old-fashioned melodrama, you felt he would have done had he possessed them. Altogether we were pleased with him and Vladimir was delighted that his trip had not been in vain.

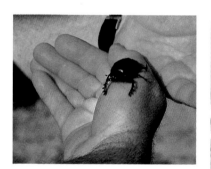

Dung beetles are the cleaning ladies of this terrain, making sure that the unruly and vulgar camels do not leave the desert in a mess. Cleaning up after camels not only keeps the desert tidy, of course, but provides cosy nurseries and larders for lots of baby dung beetles.

A little way from where we had our trying time attempting to film the reptiles, we found an additional bonus. A thoughtful passing dromedary had deposited a large pile of dung among the saxual bushes and this manna had attracted the attention of every dung beetle in Repetek. The area resembled London Airport (with no traffic control) as the huge beetles came blundering in, their wings making as much noise as miniature aeroplane engines. As they came in to land they would, with some difficulty, tuck their wings under their wing cases and then crash with a thump on the sand. After a moment to recover from this and collect their wits, they would set off towards the dung, heads down, backs humped, scuttling across the sand like strange clockwork toys. Their behaviour when they found the dung was very curious. They would bite it into sizeable chunks but did not mould it. They would then push it away across the sand, using their hind limbs and therefore travelling backwards, and during this process the dung would assume a roughly ball-like shape, thus facilitating the whole process. About five or six yards from where the dung had been collected, they would stop and dig a hole with great speed, shovelling the sand out with their behinds, like miniature blue-black bulldozers. In many instances they found either the situation wrong or maybe the temperature of the sand wrong, because after digging strenuously for a while they would abandon their burrow, grab their ball of dung and rush off to a new spot to repeat the process. Newly arrived beetles would crash land and then gallop off across the sand towards the dung pile, but if en route they encountered another beetle busily toting his dung ball, the new arrival would attack, wrest the ball away and depart triumphantly with its stolen booty. Their sense of smell must be extraordinary for the dung must have been deposited at some time before dawn, as it had dried out considerably and there was – from our point of view – no smell from it. Yet, looking around, you could see beetles homing in on it from two to three hundred yards away. Standing by this dung pile with these buzzing beetles converging on you from all directions really made you feel like a careless Gulliver occupying the flight path of a Lilliputian air force.

This day the director decided to show us how the staff normally patrolled the reserve – on camelback. It was easier and cheaper than a vehicle but infinitely more uncomfortable. Three moaning, slouching, flat-footed dromedaries were assembled and we climbed on to them. I could quite see what the director meant when he said it was the most suitable form of transport for the desert. To begin with it did not require petrol, but simply refuelled itself at each bush it passed. Secondly, it could travel across places that would defeat a vehicle. Thirdly, once you got used to the curious swaying motion on top of the flattened, slightly square saddle, you could swivel round and sit backwards, so you could talk to your friends behind you. Fourthly, you had enough space on the saddle to brew up a pot of tea or even cook a simple meal, and fifthly, he pointed out as we came to a stop and the camel knelt, you could sit in the shade of your camel – which is what we proceeded to do. The camels in a group cast quite a lot of shade, and they lay there moaning, gnashing their yellow teeth, uttering bubbling

Moving round the reserve on camels is the most sensible means of progression, if one is not prone to seasickness. The camels, though unlovely and complaining beasts, can saunter over the huge harkhans, where most vehicles would falter and fail, snatching sustenance from each passing bush and treating the huge drifting dunes as if they were smooth motorways.

In spite of the temperatures and the somewhat uninviting habitat, the desert abounded in birds. The white-winged spotted woodpecker (far left) and the bee-eater (left) were two of the more colourful of the desert inhabitants. The crested larks (below left) made the mornings melodic with their lovely song, while at night the owls (below right) flew on silent wings in search of prey, occasionally uttering tremulous cries.

The Pander's ground jay (above) is an anomaly. Unlike other jays, it refuses to live in trees and spends most of its life running about on the ground, as if it were an ostrich or some other flightless bird.

cries of protest in the way that camels do, while we discussed the mysteries of the great dunes of the Karakum.

The face of the desert was a wonderful page of nature to read, for it was really a sort of sand diary. Here were the long-humped burrows created by the light-mahogany-coloured cockroach (a most antedeluvian-looking creature). Here was a turbulent star in the sand decorated with feathers, to tell you where a hawk had appeared magically out of a clear sky and driven its talons into some small bird, pinning it to the dune. Here was a daisy-chain of delicate footprints donated by a toad-headed lizard. Here was the front door of a small rodent's residence and near it – at a discreet distance – its tiny lavatory of pellets, like a neat pile of buckshot. Here was a half-dead saxual tree, its withered arthritic limbs forming the ideal springboard for a roller, blue and emerald-green, who hawked the desert insects and left a gleaming pile of wing cases, like fragmented jewels on the sand beneath the saxual. All these clues (enough to delight Sherlock Holmes himself) were of such absorbing interest and told such a vivid story that you almost did not need to see the animal that had contributed to this rich and complex diary.

By now it was midday and all the plant shadows, so firmly etched earlier on, had converged and been absorbed, as it were, by the roots, so now each shrub, each flower, each blade of grass had lost its shadow doppelganger and stood in the breathless heat in a tiny puddle of shade. The heat was stunning and we went back to headquarters to eat and then lie limp as lettuces on our beds and let the air conditioning freeze us into sweaty ice cubes.

The following day we were up and away early. While Lee and I watched birds, Rodney went off with Byron to film great gerbils if they could find them. The desert in the early morning was alive with birds and ringing with bird song. We saw an owl (late going to bed) being mobbed by small birds and everywhere the handsome tree sparrows, the males with black feathering like a pigtail that started at the beak and went over the head and down the neck. There were rollers and bee-eaters, decked out in greens and yellows and blues, looking freshly enamelled, hawking for the newly awakened insects still drowsy from the cool night temperatures. Then suddenly the dunes around us were filled with harsh squawking cries, which suddenly turned into the most magical liquid song, rich and deep and melodious. It seemed incredible that one bird could be responsible for the two sounds, they were at such variance with each other. However, searching the saxual grove carefully with my binoculars, I suddenly found him, a golden oriole, bright as a nugget against the green of the saxual leaves. As I watched him, he threw back his head again and the beautiful liquid song filled the air.

At this point Rodney and Byron reappeared, full of excitement. They had not only located the gerbil colony and filmed it, but had also filmed what Rodney claimed was a marbled polecat, a very rare creature I had long wanted to see. However, knowing that poor Rodney was no naturalist, I did not pin a lot of faith on this. But, whatever he had filmed, it sounded most interesting, especially as he had seen it carrying a dead gerbil to its den, which implied that it had babies there. We decided that the following day we would get up before dawn and get out into the desert while everything was just waking up. Rodney would set up the camera and film this mystery beast for as long as was necessary. He would then send Byron back to fetch us to see it. This we did, setting off in a pale apricot and mauve sunrise, travelling over dunes dark with dew, to a sleepy, tentative dawn chorus of birds – like an orchestra tuning up – which swelled to a crescendo as the sun slid up above the horizon. We waited an hour or so and then Byron appeared in great spirits to tell us that the creatures did indeed have

young and that Rodney had got film of the adults with the babies and one parent bringing a gerbil to feed them. Furthermore, Byron said, they were so bold and inquisitive that we did not have to worry about noise or concealing ourselves. This proved to be true, for we found Rodney in a small valley squatting on the sand in the open. In front of him, twenty feet away, was an old black saxual, twisted and gnarled, with a great pile of dead trunks and branches about its base. Around this were several old gerbil holes. As we approached Rodney, we saw the mystery animal. It was a least weasel, who slid out of the undergrowth and stood up, straight as a ruler, watching us with deep interest and displaying no symptoms of alarm. He had a beautiful bronze-reddish coat, slightly darker on the muzzle, tail and paws. We sat down on the sand and the weasel watched us for a bit but then, presumably deciding we were too immobile to be of any interest, he suddenly vanished like a puff of brown smoke down one of the old gerbil holes. As he disappeared his mate and babies made their entrance like a troupe of medieval tumblers, scampering up and down the saxual tree, leaping and slithering through the branches with such agility and speed that we were bewildered and had difficulty in following them with our eyes. It seemed to me that the female weasel, when pregnant, had picked out a very suitable nursery in amongst the accumulated brushwood round the old saxual. It was an ideal site for three reasons: the brushwood gave them protection and any number of escape routes, the saxual gave them shade; and, finally, on their doorstep was a gerbil colony to act as a sort of living larder. It was, from the weasels' point of view, an eminently suitable and satisfactory home.

Right and opposite: *The great gerbil, an enchanting rodent, is a vital food source for the predators of the desert. Owls and hawks, desert monitors and snakes depend on it, as does the least weasel. The least weasel* (top and above), *a dapper, lithe little animal, lives a rapid and quicksilver life, as we soon found out when we tried to film a family group. They moved so fast that at the end of an hour we were all quite bewildered trying to follow their circus-like acrobatics.*

BAIKAL
Seals and sables

БАЙКАЛ

BAIKAL

Above: *The people of Buryat are Tibetan in appearance and wear wonderfully colourful local costumes.*

Preceding page: *Lake Baikal and (inset) a Baikal ornul, a most delicious fish, found only in Baikal, which tastes like slightly sweet salmon and has the advantage of being equally delectable eaten raw, smoked, or poached.*

To get to Lake Baikal from Moscow took us seventeen hours and we passed through five time zones before we arrived in Ulan-Ude, more dead than alive. However, we soon forgot our exhaustion, for looking out of the hotel bedroom window, we got the curious impression that we had arrived by mistake in Tibet. We were now in the Buryat Republic and the Buryats have eyes like animated black olives in wonderful faces with high cheekbones, generous mouths, carefully sculpted, and skins the colour of early peaches with a flush of ripeness on the cheekbones, a sort of natural rouge for both men and women. They are gay, friendly, exuberant people, putting their arms round one another, laughing and joking in the streets in a way that I am sure would have been completely alien to the Muscovites.

We had two days to wait in Ulan-Ude, for, owing to bad weather, the big chopper could not fly us down the lake to the Barguzin Reserve. I waited with some impatience, as Lake Baikal is a place I had always wanted to visit. Not only is it the largest and deepest body of fresh water on the planet, but it also has evolved its own specialized fauna, various crustaceans and fish, and, perhaps oddest of all, a diminutive freshwater seal that is found nowhere else in the world. At this time of year, of course, Lake Baikal was frozen over under an eight-foot layer of ice, but we had chosen this particular time to visit it because it was the season when, strangely enough, the seals were breeding. At last the weather cleared and the giant chopper could take off, carrying our entourage and our curious assortment of baggage. How curious can be judged from the cryptic label on one box, which read 'Canadian flag, Alex's pants and suspenders, bird seed'.

At first we flew over gently undulating lowlands with tiny, ash-grey shanty towns tucked between the hills, linked by thread-like roads and baby railways. On the rivers ice was beginning to break up, jigsawing their surfaces with black cracks. Gradually the hills got higher and higher, the forests striped and patched with melting snow and each high peak wearing a skull-cap of it. Then the chopper lifted over the last range of hills and before us was Lake Baikal in all its glory.

Hundreds of white snakes of river curl down to feed it and the lake itself was vast and pearly and appeared as smooth as cream. The air was crystal clear and bright with sunshine and fifty miles away you could see the further shore, mountains hunched under rugs of snow, pinkish in the sunlight. Then we flew over what the Russians call 'The Nose' (what a misnomer), a range of small mountains joined to the mainland by a narrow isthmus. These greeny-black mountains looked like a series of rather lumpy pillows on which somebody had spread a lace shawl of snow with a fringe. As we flew closer and our perspective changed so did the snow patterns, and then it looked as if someone

At the unusual outdoor museum in Ulan-Ude, various types of old house are preserved and the attendants dress in national costume. Amusingly, the attendant on the left was one over the eight and fell off his horse moments after this photo was taken.

We visited a fascinating place where the ancient Buryat art of the silversmith has been successfully revived, and the most exquisite jewellery and other ornaments are made. For me this was a most expensive visit as Lee has a passion for silver, but the silversmith seemed delighted we had called.

Of particular interest at the museum were the lovely carved and painted shutters, which make the log cabins so charming.

had taken the dark canvas of the mountains and painted on them with snow white filigrees and delicate trees, flowers and undulating seaweeds. As we flew along it, it was like a gigantic ever-changing mural that was quite breathtaking in its beauty. As we flew lower and lower over the surface of the lake, you could see that what appeared to be so smooth in the distance was in fact uneven, for the ice was patterned with old blurred splits in its surface and clean razor slashes of new cracks; now was the beginning of the great thaw that would soon turn Baikal into a sparkling inland sea.

We flew low over the ice and landed in the normal flurry of snow and twigs on the outskirts of the reserve. Here we found that we would share the director's house. He had kindly divided up his large living room with a curtain so that we would have a bedroom and a living room area while he, poor man, had to camp out in his young daughter's bedroom. It was typical of the hospitality that we received all over the Soviet Union and no amount of protesting on our part would alter it. They were kindly adamant. If we were going to see their country and film it, they were determined to give us the best possible treatment.

The following day we went out in a convoy of four jeeps and two cars to try to find female seals and their young. At this time of the year it could be quite hazardous driving over the lake, as the surface was just starting to break up. In the leading jeep we had the most experienced man, who could find our way across the now splitting ice that was being dismembered by the sun and judge how dangerous it was to jump a crevasse. For some distance we drove along the shore and then when we wanted to go out into the middle of the lake to the seals' breeding grounds we found we were penned in, as it were, by a very large split in the ice. Our leading jeep dashed to and fro trying to find a way round it

It was the beginning of the great thaw and so in some places the snow was beginning to melt, forming lace-like patterns on the hills that were quite exquisite. These hillsides were at the edge of the enormous Lake Baikal, forming a sort of picture frame round this huge body of frozen water. We flew over the lake where the ice had cracked and then been healed by a fresh layer, leaving the surface criss-crossed with scars.

The view from the little house we lived in at the headquarters of Barguzin Reserve, looking out onto the vast expanse of the lake.

Opposite: When the ice splits, it sounds like an enormous cannonade, a boom that echoes over the lake and makes the ice shudder. As the new ice starts to form in these cracks, you hear the song of the lake, the musical noises by 'baby' ice forming and being crushed and re-forming again.

but the split was too long and so there was only one thing to do and that was to jump it. As these new splits occur (deafening as a cannonade), new ice starts to form like a second skin growing over a wound, and this is the danger. Before you jump one of the crevasses, you must first test the quality of the ice with a spade and a curious instrument that is vaguely reminiscent of an assegai. If the new ice proves to be firm enough, you can jump it.

Finally it was decided at which point it was safe enough for us to try a crossing and we circled round and took a run at it, kangarooing over not just one but three large crevasses in the ice. Having successfully achieved this, the leading jeep dashed off ahead to ferret out further hazards and we followed sedately in the rear. You can read the ice almost like a weather map or at any rate a sort of diary of how the weather has been. Here the wind whipped up waves that promptly froze; here the sun melted the ice in the misshapen potholes or pools and these froze too; here the ice had split, jagged as a shaft of lighting, and was being healed by the formation of new ice, fragile and delicate as a church window and, as it is subjected to the heat of the sun, the movements of the water below and the uneasy shrugging of the vast ice overcoat the lake wears, you become conscious of the most extraordinary noises. While waiting for the lead jeep to pathfind for us, I got out of our vehicle and approached one of these great wounds in the ice that was being healed by new ice growth. I found that as this baby ice forms and is subjected to these various pressures, it sets up an orchestration of protest. It tinkles like tiny cymbals, it purrs like a basketful of cats, it trills like a summer bank of crickets and ticks like a shop-full of

One of the great enchantments of Lake Baikal in the winter is that you can drive over it in jeeps.

Preceding pages: Everywhere you looked on Baikal the snow and the ice had combined to make the most flamboyant and beautiful arrangement that any modern sculptor would envy. At one point the ice had seized a wrecked ship and gilded it with snow and ice, turning it into a work of art. At another place, a dead tree had been turned into a Christmas cake decoration, bedecked with icicles.

clocks. This is, in fact, the symphony of Lake Baikal, a lake being re-born, emerging from its sarcophagus of ice and singing as it does so.

Not long after this, far out in the centre of the lake, we found a seal's nursery, a hole in the thick ice that is vital to the animal, for through it it gets up to breathe and through it it returns in order to fish. These holes are kept open by the seals using teeth and claws. When the female is ready to breed she constructs a small ice palace near the hole in which she gives birth to her baby and in which the infant lives until it is weaned. The ice palace we found was very beautiful, for the rucked-up ice and snow gleamed sapphire-blue in the sun and the entrance was armed with icicles, so that it looked like the gaping mouth of a shark. Unfortunately, there was no baby in the ice palace for us to film, but we had the most amusing picnic. Two cars were backed up to each other, long wooden planks were produced and these were run from bumper to bumper to form both the table and the seats. In a moment the table was covered with piles of tinned salmon and sprats and fresh, slightly salted fish called omul, which were delicious. This was served with cartwheels of fresh brown bread and huge jars of home-made pickles. To accompany this there was tea in vast quantities, which was brewed by the simple expedient of filling a bucket full of snow, hanging it on a tripod and getting the water to boiling point by aiming a huge bunsen burner at it. I think it must have been one of the most unusual picnics I have ever had, sitting on eight feet of ice, with a mile of water straight down beneath it, on the heart of the biggest lake in the world.

We continued our search for baby seals but to no avail, and as the shadows were growing purple and black in the twilight, we drove back across that enormous pie-crust of ice to the reserve. On the way we

found a place where a bear had been crossing the frozen lake from one peninsula to another and had left lovely fat tracks firm and deep in the snow like huge Elizabethan seals on white parchment.

The next day we had many things to accomplish. One of the success stories of the Barguzin Reserve is its great contribution to the survival of the sable. For years this lovely animal was hunted for its magnificent coat and hunted indiscriminately. Its numbers dwindled and the animal teetered on the borders of extinction until suddenly its plight was realized and a ban on hunting was introduced. Gradually, with the aid of this protection and a captive breeding programme, the sable population recovered from its precarious state and is no longer in danger. As I had never met one of these animals, I was delighted when the director of the reserve informed me that he had caught one especially for us to film. It was, in fact, an animal that had been ear tagged (an operation rather like ringing a bird) and had been captured three times in five years in a square half-mile of forest. People who complain about zoos have little knowledge of what circumscribed lives most animals live. If they find what is needful for them in a tiny area, they become as parochial as an English villager.

Our sable was established in a splendid, large, aviary-like structure filled with hollow logs, in which he had taken up residence with such nonchalance that I felt sure he was getting quite used to being on intimate terms with human beings. However, they had made the mistake of feeding him too lavish a meal (meat, liver and raw egg) and

The streams, kept ice-free by thermal springs miles away in the hills, had to force their way into the lake through a shark's jaw of icicles.

Our enchanting if bad-tempered sable star. The Barguzin Reserve played a major role in saving this enchanting animal from extinction. Overhunted for its fur, its numbers had dropped dramatically. With careful conservation the population increased, and small quantities were exported to found new colonies in other Soviet reserves. Now the population has risen to between 1000 and 1500. I still stick to my view that only a sable deserves to wear a sable coat.

he was busy sleeping it off in a hollow log and saw no reason for disturbing his siesta in order to appear on television. It took a lot of persuasion, a lot of chivvying and a lot of blocking up of hollow logs before we could get him to agree to take part in the show and even then he said some extremely derogatory and insulting things to Lee and me for having disturbed his afternoon nap. Fortunately, he said all these things in sablese, in which we were not versed, so that his more unpleasant comments were lost on us.

He was an enormously elegant beast, with a strange pale little coffee-coloured face with big dark eyes and a boot-button nose shiny as a blackberry. He had wonderful furry upstanding ears like arum lilies that somehow made him look like a charming Victorian young lady, all eager eyes and a winter-polished nose in an elegant poke bonnet. His fur was a wonderful sort of smoky-red and so finely wrought that it was easy to see why it is the most expensive fur in the world, though how anyone has the heart to kill such a charming beast in order to remove its skin is a mystery to me.

Having successfully filmed the sable and released it, we received

Two-and-a-half months old, this young Baikal seal – just out of its white baby coat – behaved in front of the cameras in an impeccable manner, upstaging Lee in every scene as the young Shirley Temple used to do to her co-stars and adding point to the adage that if you want to be a star on screen, don't act with an animal or a child. At the turn of the century, owing to overhunting, there were probably less than 5000 Baikal seals left. However, strict protection has had the satisfactory result that now the numbers have risen to 75,000 animals, a marvellous example of what wise conservation can accomplish.

the welcome news that they had found a baby Baikal seal and, as it were, retained its services for the film. The baby had already been transported to a suitable area of the lake and was now awaiting our pleasure. So once more our caravan of jeeps went shuddering and bumping and jumping over the ice until we reached the spot where our seal film star was awaiting us. When we opened the box that was acting as a dressing room for our co-star, a delightful sight met our eyes. A fat baby seal, some two feet long, with grey and black blotched fur, huge quivering whiskers, a nose like a small black velvet pincushion and melting brown eyes as big as mulberries stared up at us soulfully. We immediately christened it Olga, a fine Russian name that seemed to suit it. At first she was a little fearful and inclined to snap, but after a short time she decided that this strange mob of humans meant no harm and became besotted with us. We wanted her to go off among the ice palaces and behave like a true seal, but she insisted on flopping about on the ice, following us everywhere and lying on our feet as if she were a domestic dog. Only when we dug a hole in the ice that she could swim in did she start taking her acting career seriously and then she had a scene with Lee in which she upstaged my wife unmercifully, flopping about with melting eyes, plunging in and out of the pool and finally lying on her back, her fat tummy stuck up, waving her flippers in the air with gay abandon. Towards the end, however, Olga began to get bored with this acting nonsense and she started to yawn. So we took her out to an ice palace and a nice hole in the ice and let her go. The animal that had appeared so ungainly on the ice slid into the water like quicksilver and vanished into the clear depths in a burst of bubbles.

The scene stealer

This page and overleaf: *Should you feel the pangs of hunger on Lake Baikal, all you have to do is to chip a hole in the ice (a process that keeps you warm and increases your appetite), drop your fishing line into the gin-clear waters and catch fish for your lunch.*

When the edges of the ice hole have been baited with grubs, you watch for the fish to rise. They virtually jump onto the hook, giving you a substantial catch in no time.

Some of the three hundred-odd rivers that feed Lake Baikal remain free from ice because they are born of hot springs. The helicopter flew us in to examine this phenomenon. Here the hot sulphurous water, real volcano blood, welled from the Earth and hot as bathwater, started its journey to the lake. The helicopter was supposed to come back in an hour to collect us but, as always happens when you are miles from civilization, it had engine trouble and so it was four hours later that we were rescued. The crew found Lee and me asleep like babes in the wood, though, unlike the fairy tale, we were very stiff, cold and disgruntled.

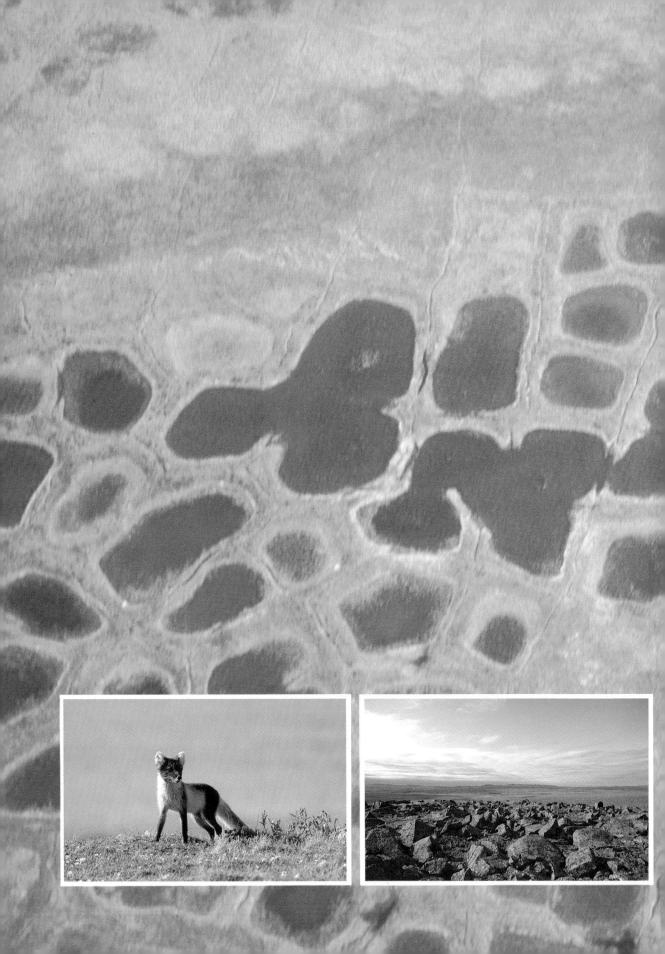

TAYMYR
The endless day

ТАЙМЫР
TAYMYR

Busy, beautiful and belligerent, the lemmings swarm over the tundra and in this bleak environment form an important source of food for the predators. Without lemmings trotting down their highways through the moss there would be no hawks, no owls and no arctic foxes.

Preceding page insets: *The spongy tundra gives way to screes of grey-black slate on the western side of Lake Taymyr (left). An arctic fox (far left).*

Preceding page and opposite: *The Taymyr tundra was an extraordinary landscape, for the multitude of ponds was like a gigantic shattered mirror, and in places where the ice had pushed up the surface of the tundra, it looked almost like a series of man-made fields, like the rice fields in the Far East. Over the higher tundra the ground was more undulating, and caught in the curves of these low hills were swathes of snow as yet unmelted even by the constant sun.*

THE Taymyr Peninsula stretches some 750 miles above the Arctic Circle and ends less than a thousand from the North Pole. This is the tundra, a completely different terrain from any we had been in on our journey. It was a long and uncomfortable flight from Moscow, during which we passed through four time zones before reaching the land of the midnight sun. We landed at Khatanga and were met by the local television representative, a pleasant, quiet man, who gave us the most sumptuous lunch in this tiny town that looks like a frontier town in the gold rush days. Then, replete, we stowed our baggage away in the helicopter and took off for the Bikada Reserve, which lay some 350 miles north of the town, as remote as the moon.

The tundra was weird and magnificent, a flat, green-gold land with thousands of gleaming lakelets and ponds of the most astonishing shapes and sizes. Some were like tadpoles, some like birds, many like pendulums, squares or isosceles triangles, all a deep blue, almost black. Here and there you could see great ribs and half-moons of unmelted snow, although it was supposed to be midsummer, and in places you could see where the winter ice had shouldered up the tundra, forming ridges so regular that in certain parts they looked like the borders of man-made fields. The atmosphere was crystal clear and the sky a rich blue under the perpetual sun. It was extraordinary looking out on to the brilliantly lit landscape to think that you could not tell whether it was midday or midnight.

Now the tundra became more undulating, greeny-yellow, wrinkled and ruffled like a velvet tablecloth draped over the hills, and the lakes had shawls of half-melted snow on their dark, mirror-like surfaces. Eventually we flew low over a wide fast-flowing river, the Bikada, and on its banks was a small cluster of buildings, which was the headquarters of the reserve. A spot more removed from civilization would be hard to imagine, but the clear air, the sunshine and the wonderful silence (once the helicopter had departed) made it a magical place. We were billeted in a tiny house of three rooms, which all eight of us had to inhabit. It was comfortable enough but the most distracting thing was the constant sunlight. It actually had – until we got used to it – as unsettling an effect as jet lag. But with the aid of that indispensable product gaffer tape we managed to stick up blankets and coats over the windows so that our rooms were steeped in gloom, and Lee soon learnt to sleep with a sock tied over her eyes, which made her look like the bride of Frankenstein, but achieved night where no night was.

Outside in the sunshine was an extraordinary green world of its own. The first four or five inches under your feet were spongy and soft, like a multicoloured pile carpet formed by the plants and miniature trees that grew there. Beneath, the ground was frozen. Dig your fingers

164

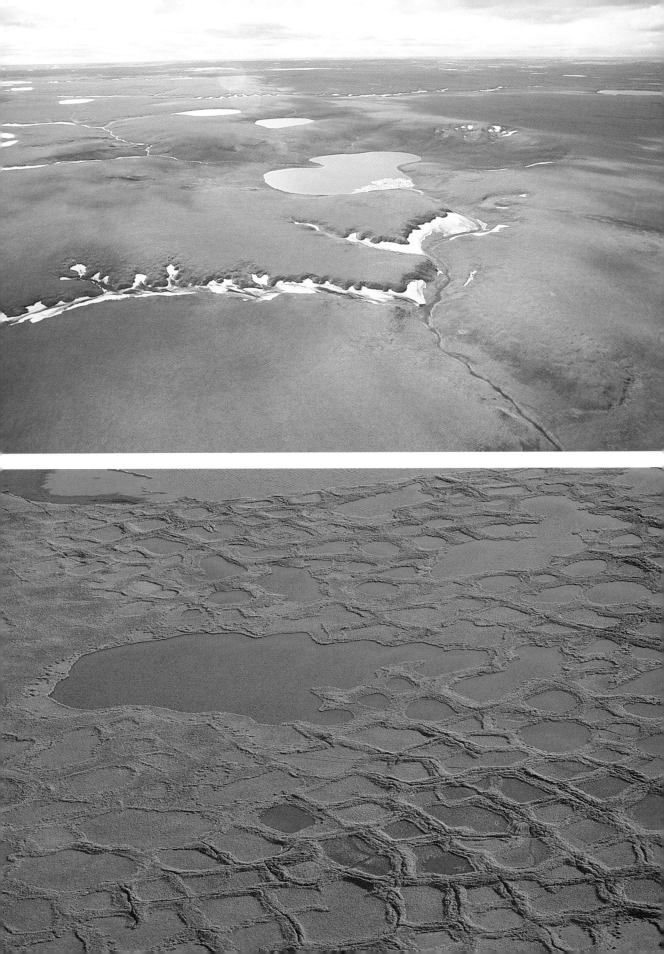

This page and opposite: *Everything here was miniature, the trees only knee high, the plants and lovely flowers so miniscule you had to go down on hands and knees to appreciate their beauty. In this harsh environment everything has to be tiny, for being small is a form of protection against the elements.*

down through the moss as you would do through the fur of an animal and it was as if you had dipped them into a deep-freeze. You were, in effect, walking on a thick soft rug'of moss and herbs laid over a floor of frozen earth. There were fuzzy little daisy-like flowers and others, madonna-blue, like miniature forget-me-nots, shining up at you. Everywhere there were ankle high forests of dwarf willow, with pink flowers like muffs, growing sturdily in the emerald-green layer of moss. Between the great pincushions of moss and the baby forests ran roadways, stamped out by the busy feet of the lemmings.

Our chief filming objective in the tundra was the musk ox. This strange, shaggy, stocky animal was once common in the Siberian tundra, yet died out in the rest of Siberia some ten thousand years ago, lingering on in Taymyr until three thousand years ago, judging by fossil remains. When they became extinct is a mystery, but one theory is that the climate changed and made it unsuitable for them. However, I think this theory may not hold water, since the reintroduction of musk ox seems to be working well. In the 1930s the Soviet authorities decided that musk ox should once again roam on the tundra, so they tried to buy some animals from Greenland. Negotiations were protracted and before the animals could be shipped, the war started, which put paid to the whole scheme. After the war nothing much happened until President Trudeau of Canada was visiting the Soviet Union and learnt of their musk-ox-less state and offered them ten animals as a gift. Not to be outdone in zoological diplomacy the United States offered fifty oxen. These shaggy gifts duly arrived; some

were sent to Wrangel Island in the Polar Sea and thirty were sent to Taymyr. Here they prospered and the total number on the two-million-acre reserve is now 104 beasts.

When we had landed we had been greeted by Gregory, who was, as it were, father to the musk ox, for it was he who had gone to fetch them and it was he who had travelled recently to a conference in Fairbanks to proudly announce the success of the reintroduction, which many scientists had said was doomed to failure. Gregory had a brown, humorous face; at the mere mention of musk ox, his face would light up and it was obvious that these creatures were the most important things in his life. He told us that he was sure we could get film of the oxen since he could have them rounded up for us with a dog. The whole thing sounded so bizarre that I had little faith in it, but we thought that we might as well try.

The next day the chopper arrived and we took off, carrying with us the musk ox dog, a small Siberian husky called Deke, a handsome creature who treated the whole thing with great aplomb and was obviously quite used to this extraordinary method of hunting. I must say that I was more excited than Deke because for some reason I have a passion for musk ox and one of my ambitions was to see them in the wild. It had all come about because I once met a baby one in Copenhagen Zoo which was so enchanting that I fell deeply in love with the species. Now this prospect of seeing real, wild musk ox on the tundra was most exciting.

We flew some way over the gently undulating hills, green and gold in the sunshine, the numerous ponds and lakes flashing like fish scales as we passed. Then we banked and started to go down, and immediately Deke began to take an interest in the proceedings. He got up off the floor and went to one of the windows, pressing his nose against it and studying the ground intently. Suddenly his whole body became tense and he started to whine and give throaty little barks, and below us we saw the musk ox herd. We dropped lower and lower until we were right behind them. Deke was now going wild, barking and uttering yodelling howls of excitement. The oxen galloped before us, shaggy as old hearth rugs, with pale muzzles and their curved horns looking like the bleached branches you find washed up on remote shorelines. As they galloped, their cream-coloured stumpy legs thumped the bare ground between the moss patches and raised a miniature dust storm. We came in lower and lower behind them and by now Deke was hysterical with excitement. We were still some six feet from the ground when the helicopter door was opened and Deke zoomed out, like a greyhound out of a trap in pursuit of his quarry. He sped across the tundra, soon overtook the lumbering musk ox and ran round and round them, barking like a maniac. The musk ox then indulged in the classic musk ox manoeuvre. They formed a circle, babies in the middle, all adults with their fearsome horns pointing outward in a bristling and intimidating barrier. The major bull of the herd – if Deke got too close – would suddenly break the circle and charge him, massive head down, the great scythe of his horns ready to spit the unfortunate dog, but Deke was too agile and too clever to be caught thus and would dance

Opposite: *The tundra is really like a huge green sponge laid on a block of ice. The hummocks as you walk over them feel like a thick pile carpet, and in between them you can see the little roads formed by the lemmings.*

out of the bull's way. After much head tossing and irritated snorting the bull would return to the circle only to be enticed out once more by his infuriation at Deke's daring. It was an impressive sight to see these powerful animals standing shoulder to shoulder in a circle, their horns forming an impregnable fence behind which their young were safely guarded.

We filmed them for some time and then we struck a snag. As long as Deke was barking at them they maintained their defensive posture, but if he was called off the herd immediately lumbered away, so it was impossible to get any footage of them behaving naturally, as it were. After several futile attempts to solve this problem we decided to try to find the other herd to see if they would be more amenable. We eventually found them but they proved to be just as uncooperative, either forming a defensive circle with much horn rattling or else galloping over the horizon with considerable speed and determination. We eventually did solve the problem but more by accident than by design.

We had gone down the river in a flotilla of boats in order to film a particularly beautiful hillock of wild flowers we had found. Just before we reached our destination, however, at a place where the rolling hills were perhaps two or three hundred feet high, we saw a whole herd of musk ox like a black frieze against the blue sky, browsing placidly, some lying down in deep slumber, others feeding their babies. Gregory explained that he had buried a lot of rock salt here and the oxen came to this manufactured salt lick from time to time. We eased the boats into the banks and the crew set off up the hillside in an attempt to film the oxen behaving naturally. In this they were successful, getting some nice footage of the young suckling, the older ones dozing among the flowers, and others digging for and licking at the salt. Then Rodney decided he wanted a piece of action that would match in with the stuff

My first sight of wild musk ox (opposite) was a very thrilling moment, though I still don't know why I am so enamoured of the weird, uncombed-looking beasts. Once they form their defensive circle (above), bristling with horns, it would take a very brave predator to try to broach the circle to get at the young ones within.

Top: *The musk ox, languidly grazing, sleeping and feeding at the artificial salt lick, had a rude awakening when Byron did his famous dog imitation. Owing to the success of a Soviet reintroduction programme, there are now over a hundred musk ox living in Taymyr.* Above: *Deke, our musk ox hound, here takes on a lone bull and is driven into the river. Deke's eyesight was extraordinary and he could spot a herd of oxen from the helicopter even before we could and would go mad with delight, for his favourite sport was rounding up these massive shaggy beasts.*

he had already shot, so he got Byron (world famous for his animal impressions) to crawl further up the hill until he was near the herd and then give an imitation of Deke in a frenzy, and this he did. It says much for Byron's imitative prowess as well as for Deke's reputation that with the first yelp the musk ox panicked. Those that had been sleeping leapt to their feet, those that had been browsing ceased at once. Babies were bundled together and the defensive circle was hurriedly formed in spite of the fact that no human or dog was visible to the animals. The poor creatures must have been greatly puzzled when no Deke appeared, but we were jubilant since it meant we had got all the musk ox material we needed and could now concentrate on our next two objectives, to get film of reindeer and the red-breasted geese, probably one of the most beautiful of all waterfowl.

According to our oracle, Gregory, the birds were nesting on an island where the Bikada River joins Lake Taymyr, one of the largest lakes in the world. This was where he proposed to take us, for as well as red-breasted geese, there was a host of different birds that used the island as a nesting site. We set off early in our armada of boats. I could tell it was early only by looking at my watch, for the sun had been shining brightly all night as usual. We found it was as easy to film at four o'clock in the morning as it was to film at midday, for the light was perfect, but we did find that this constant sunlight had a disorientating effect.

The island lay some four or five miles from the headquarters where the river flowed out and was lost in the vastness of the lake. The island, when we came to it, proved to be about a mile long by half a mile wide. It was surrounded by beaches and dunes of grey sand, but above this the spongy covering of moss and baby willows was broken by hundreds of little ponds that made it an ideal nesting site for every species of bird, protected from foxes by the fast-flowing river, lush with water plants and insects, with placid shallow pools where fragile babies could learn to swim and hunt for food. That the island was an enormous nursery became apparent to us as we breasted the small grey cliffs and saw the air explode with alarmed birds in a great snowstorm of white wings. Glaucous gulls and herring gulls wheeled over us like some strange mobile caught in a hurricane, each bird honking, bleating or mewing abuse at us. The black-headed sabine gulls were even more belligerent and, as soon as we ventured to walk inland, dive-bombed us unmercifully, one swooping down on me and coming so close that the wind from his wings actually parted my hair. Flocks of dark chocolate-coloured female eider ducks flew past us, their rapidly moving wings making a noise like someone ripping a sheet of silk apart. The eider drake must consider a noisy crêche no place for such an elegant bird, for we saw only one drake, sailing sedately along, a wonderful sight with his white breast, green head and black mask, a most aristocratic-looking duck with a very supercilious expression. He obviously felt that, having mated, he had justified his existence and wanted nothing further to do with squawking young. We were impressed by the number of species we saw, stints, Lapland longspurs, jaegers and red- and black-throated divers, but we forgot them all because suddenly a skein of red-breasted geese swooped across the sky in black silhouette, and then, as they turned, displayed their wonderful coloration – the white flash on their beaks, the glossy black and white of their bodies, and the lovely brick-red pinkish colour of the cheeks and breast. We waited for them to settle and then cautiously approached their nests, some of which had young and some of which had eggs. They were extraordinarily trustful and allowed us to approach within ten feet of them while they either manipulated their tiny young into the pools for swimming lessons or else snuggled more tightly over their eggs. What magnificent birds they were, as they wheeled across the sky, their red breasts glinting in the sun, uttering choruses of plaintive, honking cries like groups of wounded basoons.

We spent a wonderful day on the island filming and bird watching, which was just as well, for on the following day the whole tundra as far as the eye could see was under a sheet of cloud as black and viscous as

A red-breasted goose, probably the world's most beautiful waterfowl, turning into the sun to show its wonderful terracotta colouring.

This island was, of course, an ideal nesting site for red-breasted geese, and there were plenty of them, some sitting on eggs and some teaching their lovely fluffy young to swim in the tiny ponds that dotted the island. These geese nest only in the Soviet Union and are classified as an endangered species.

tar. A cold rain fell, made all the cooler by a biting wind that drove it like flails. You became suddenly very conscious of the fact that you were, in effect, living on a gigantic ice cube covered with a thin layer of vegetation. There was nothing we could do for two days except huddle for warmth in every stitch of clothing we possessed, and play Trivial Pursuit, a riotous game that Byron had had the good sense to bring with him. On the third day with a feeble glimmer of sun, Rodney, never one to take to inactivity kindly, decided he must film lemmings. The fact that we did not have any of these tiny rodents did not deter him in the least. He enlisted the aid of Deke and another dog, and he, John and Byron went off into the soggy tundra and, to our astonishment, returned in an hour or so with two adult and three baby lemmings, which we housed in three coolers, the small plastic refrigerators that the film is packed in. They settled down quite placidly and proved to be enchanting beasts. The adults were about five inches long, fat, low to the ground, with neat little paws, brilliant brown eyes and round ears almost buried in their thick fur. The top parts were a rich rufous-red, flecked with black and with a black stripe running from the top of the head to the ridiculous little stumpy tail. The babies – all three of which would have fitted comfortably into a tea cup – were delightful, with

Where the rivers, like strange green tree roots, wind down to Lake Taymyr, they embrace sections of land and form islands. These islands, protected from marauding arctic foxes by their fast-flowing river 'moats', form ideal sanctuaries on which a myriad of birds breed unmolested.

chubby faces, bright eyes and neatly manicured little feet. Their backs were a paler rufous than the adults' and with no black flecks, but the black stripe from head to stumpy tail was very pronounced. They were extremely self-possessed and, though the adults would try to bite if you picked them up, the young merely uttered faint ladylike squeaks, like elderly spinsters who had been unexpectedly pinched by the vicar. They really were the most cooperative creatures and did everything we wanted them to do. Finally, when we released them so Rodney could get some shots of them walking down their highway, they really hammed it up, sitting up and washing their faces, sniffing at flowers, pausing for a snack of willow before finally sauntering off down their highway into the tundra.

The following day the weather cleared and the helicopter came to take us on the next and last leg of our journey to a camp on the Logata River in the enormous reserve at the western edge of Lake Taymyr. Our quarry there was the vast reindeer herds that at that time were undertaking their seasonal migration towards the sea. It was a wonderful flight down the full length of this vast lake, stopping once so we could film some of the spectacular scenery. Parts of the lake were still covered in great slabs of dirty grey melting ice like soap suds on

Infinitely more attractive than a hamster, it is curious that the lemming has not been turned into a domestic pet.

the dark water. The scenery was very different from Bikada, no longer only smoothly rounded hills, but quite high escarpments with here and there screes of greyish-black slate-like rocks. Dozens of small rivers ran down to feed the lake, coiling through the green tundra like the tentacles of a silver octopus. Dotted about were strange sandy hillocks, pale fawn in colour and of the weirdest shape. At one spot, three of them alongside each other looked astonishingly like the top halves and the tails of three huge vein-tailed goldfish. The shores of the Taymyr are dotted with thousands of ponds and small lakelets that underwent a miraculous colour change as we flew over them, one minute being pure blue, the next minute turning to glittering silver coins as the sun caught them, and then as we dropped lower turning brown. It was possible as one flew low over these sherry-coloured waters to see the bones and tusks of mammoths lying higgledy-piggledy as though preserved in amber.

At length we arrived at the camp and found that, remote as it was, every effort had been made to make us comfortable. Lee and I had a tiny wooden house (with John Hartley as a boarder sleeping on the kitchen floor), the crew lived in tents, and we had an enormous marquee that acted as a combined kitchen and dining room. For this stage of the journey we had been joined by a blonde bombshell named Natasha, with periwinkle-blue eyes and a dazzling smile, who was, we were assured, an expert on reindeer. She had a tenuous command over the English language and if she did not understand a remark made to her she would fix you with a bright blue eye and utter an explosive *'What?'* that was so intimidating you felt that if she were interrogating you, you would be forced to confess to anything. She was quite adorable and truly a mine of information on reindeer. She told us that the pattern of their behaviour was to migrate northwards towards the Arctic Ocean in the spring and summer and return at the onset of winter, crossing the tundra and taking refuge in the forests beyond its borders. At the moment the great herds were moving northwards and this was what she was going to take us to see and film.

One of the advantages of the place was that there were no trees, so you could actually get good views of the birds and not just tantalizing glimpses. The strangely-named dowitcher nested in the miniature willows and birches, as did the golden plover. Also busy rearing their young were handsome snow buntings, rock ptarmigans and the pretty little Lapland longspur. On the rocky shores the Eurasian dotterel merged so perfectly with its surroundings that it was invisible until it moved.

Above and right: *Needless to say, the birds objected to our presence as if we were two-legged arctic foxes and dive-bombed us at every opportunity when we got near their nests. The bravest and the most aggressive were the jaegers, with their long pointed tails, and the handsome Sabine's gulls, with their black heads.*

(Below and bottom left and right) *Taimyr was a wonderful area for birds, which when we were there were nesting all around us. Around the little house in which we lived, Rough-legged buzzards soared in search of lemmings, and on the islands in the river eider ducks were busy incubating their eggs or fussing over their newly hatched fuzzy broods.*

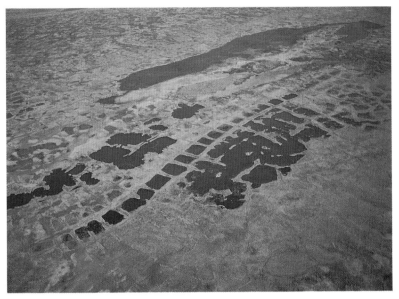

It was amazing flying over Lake Taymyr, for the landscape changed so rapidly. One minute we saw the tundra being carved up by silvery rivers that fed the lake, the next minute it was a jigsaw of melting ice, which would then turn into the strange 'paddy fields', created by the winter freezes.

The next day we set out in the helicopter and after travelling for about an hour we came upon the first herd, five or six hundred of them galloping through the valleys. Most of the females had shed their antlers and the young males had only small ones, but there were twenty or thirty mature stags with massive and beautiful horns, like huge branched winter trees shorn of their leaves, perched on their heads, rocking to and fro as the stags galloped along. The first thing that struck me was the disparity of coloration within the herds. I had always imagined that reindeer were just brown, but I soon discovered my mistake. Here were adults so dark a brown as to be almost black, others pale fawn, others reddish and some a strange silvery colour that made them look almost white. This huge conglomeration of animals, panicked by our proximity, galloped down a hill and out on to a

Top: *When we spotted them from the helicopter, the reindeer herds looked pale fawn in colour and it was only when we landed and got in amongst them that we saw the many different hues they were, and could appreciate the forest of antlers.* Above: *The snowy owl, a fierce predator, whose plumage in winter conceals him perfectly from his prey.*

comparatively flat area where there was another great herd with which they mingled, so there were several thousand animals below us, a moving carpet of colours, and here and there a forest of antlers. It was a most impressive sight, enough reindeer on the hoof to keep Father Christmas in business for many centuries.

Presently the helicopter put us down in a narrow valley, bright with flowers, where there was an outcrop of large rocks we could hide amongst. The helicopter was then going to try to gently chivvy the reindeer herds towards us so we could film them. With a stream whispering and glinting down its length, the valley was a beautiful spot, and on a grassy knoll some four hundred yards away a snowy owl stood, white as a tombstone, staring at us with astonished orange eyes. We concealed ourselves among the rocks and presently over the hill came a multicoloured flood of reindeer. Our pilot had done an excellent job, steering them into the valley without panicking them. Steadily they poured down past us, pausing now and then to graze. Sometimes a stag would gaze our way suspiciously, his massive antlers held proudly and imperiously on his head, his ears flicking to and fro to catch every sound. Gradually the vast herd went past until the last one, a magnificent stag, paused on the skyline, looked back at us and snorted as if in derision before following the herd. Cramped from

hiding behind the rocks, we rose and stretched and waited for the helicopter to come and pick us up, very pleased with this, our last day's filming in the field.

That evening we had a celebration. Instead of the endless reindeer meat we had been subsisting on, they had flown in a goose and – that rarest of things in the tundra – a salad. The last bottles of vodka and whisky were broached and many toasts drunk. Then to our astonishment and delight Natasha and the others produced an incredible present for Lee and me. When I had arrived in Taymyr, I had casually remarked that I would like a mammoth tooth as a souvenir, more in jest than in earnest, for I thought it would be impossible to obtain. Now they presented us with not simply a mammoth's tooth but one that had mounted on it a baby mammoth's tusk some two feet long, on one side of which had been carved a loving message to us both. It was a wonderful present and we were overwhelmed.

'Natasha,' I said, raising my glass, 'this is the best present we have been given in the Soviet Union, and you are the best blonde in the Soviet Union.'

'*What*?' said Natasha.

This is the mammoth tusk we could not take home as a souvenir.

MOSCOW
The other Russians

МОСКВА
MOSCOW

Above and opposite: *These are some pictures of the pet market, taken surreptitiously, since we were warned by the stall owners that taking photographs was frowned upon, and they pointed out the presence of police at the entrance to the market and made signs for us to conceal our cameras. Why the authorities should not want this lovely market either filmed or photographed is a great mystery to me for it showed more clearly than anything else we saw in the Soviet Union the people's great love of animals, surely not a trait of character of which to be ashamed.*

Preceding page: *The golden onion domes in the Kremlin.*

EXHAUSTED but at the same time exhilarated by our experiences and the knowledge that we had successfully filmed our journey, we returned to Moscow. Here we had one more task to fulfil and as is usual in the topsy turvy world of television, it was to film the first programme. What I wanted to show was the Soviet people's love of animal life. I wanted to show that in those intimidating and ugly highrise apartment blocks there lurked a whole menagerie of lovingly cared-for animals. I wanted to show the people's great love of their zoo. And, to set the seal on it, I wanted to show the 'pet market', which I believe to be unique, as I have never seen anything like it in all my travels around the world.

Let me deal with the pet market first since it was the most frustrating thing that happened to me during our long journey and the thing that filled me with the most anguish and anger. I had been told about this market by John, who had seen it on one of his reconnaissance trips, and he had given me a glowing description of it. If I wanted to show the people's love of animals, he said, this market was a must. So we wrote it into the script of the first programme.

Permission to film this market was refused. Why, I asked? Were all the animals ill-treated there? Were they all half-starved and covered with sores? No, of course they're not, was the answer. Then why could we not film? Because the place did not look very nice, we were told. Well, could I go and look at it, I asked, and afterwards write about it? Oh yes, they said, you just can't film there. So Lee and I went down to see it with John.

It was absolutely and overwhelmingly enchanting.

In the outskirts of the centre of Moscow was this huge, rambling square and it was bursting with animals and people. There were people selling fat sleepy muskrats and hamsters and white mice. There were budgerigars, pigeons and chickens by the score and fish tanks by the hundred full of rainbows of tropical fish. Everywhere you looked there was film material of the most wonderful sort, truly showing the Soviets' joy in their animals. Here was a rotund and beaming old lady with the head of a sleepy rabbit hanging out of her coat pocket, two kittens clasped to her bosom and a third one perched on her shoulder. Here were a group of men examining a tree frog with all the seriousness of a group of jewellers assessing an emerald.

Now the Soviet Union is lavish in distributing medals to its brave citizens and one gets used to the sight in Moscow and elsewhere of benevolent old gentlemen who can hardly walk for the weight of medals on their coats. But here, in the market, it was the turn of the dogs: great danes, bull mastiffs and dalmatians all wearing great aprons of medals they had won, thus proving that their progeny, lolling fat and somnolent in front of them, were worth buying.

184

Here was a man solemnly bottle-feeding a baby coypu that was standing on its hind legs, sucking away at the milk, making noises like a contented baby. There were men haggling over the price of a terrapin, ladies with tiny shovels picking up bloodworms and small shrimps for fish fanciers and putting them into paper cones made out of sheets of *Pravda*, and one octogenarian with a moustache like a forest extolling the virtues of his pond snails to a customer with a vigour that would have been excessive if they had been gold nuggets. Here, encapsulated in this rambling, slightly unkempt square, (the sort of square that holds markets all over the world) was Russia's love of nature and animals. Here people were buying everything from bulldogs to pond weed, shrimps to parakeets. The animals were in wonderful condition and obviously their owners were proud of them, and treated them lovingly. This whole square, brimming with life, was just what I wanted, but I was not allowed to film it because 'the place did not look very nice'. To say that I was infuriated is an understatement. When I go back to Moscow, the first place I shall visit is not Lenin's Tomb or the Kremlin, but the pet market, as it is the most fascinating, warm and human place in the whole capital.

However, frustrating though this was, our time in Moscow had its compensations and one of them was meeting the enchanting Olga, a young sculptress who was working at the as yet unopened Museum of Paleontology.

Olga had been chiselling away for over a year on a mural in white sandstone, some thirty feet high and 150 feet long, which depicted a whole range of prehistoric beasts. It was a breathtaking and magnificent piece of work and she was within an ace of finishing it. Bravely she allowed me to accompany her up on to the scaffolding and, chisel and hammer in hand, help her to complete the last few hairs on a woolly mammoth's trunk. I must confess my heart was in my mouth for I could not help feeling that with the first tap of my hammer and the first dig of my chisel the beautiful work, so long in the making, would come tumbling down like a spilt jigsaw puzzle. Fortunately, this did not happen so I was not pushed off the scaffolding to my death by an irate and beautiful Olga, but rewarded with a kiss instead.

We had another enchanting experience when we filmed in the Moscow Zoo. This is a very old establishment, and most of the caging was built back in the 1900s. The city has grown up round the zoo, so it is now crushed like a flower in an inadequate pot. However, in spite of the drawbacks (which could be cured by more government backing and moving the zoo to a new site) the place is run by a dedicated and wonderful team headed by Dr Vladimir Spitzin. That the team are as devoted to him as they are to the animals in their charge is obvious, and this results in an extraordinary team spirit that makes itself felt, like the warmth of a fire on a cold night, the moment you meet them all, as we had done the first time we arrived in Moscow. They had been extremely kind to John during his previous visit and very helpful with advice about our whole project. What other zoo director, for example, would offer to send his curator two thousand miles to the desert with a mixed bag of reptiles to ensure that we did not come away empty?

What other zoo director would try to get me and my wife strangled by an octopus? What other zoo director would try to get us eaten by walrus, devoured by cheetahs — only the incomparable Spitzin. But all these excitements lay in the future. When we first reached Moscow I wanted to meet all our kind friends at the zoo and they laid on a dinner for us. It was a most convivial affair and, with the aid of Marina, Dr Spitzin's lovely and talented translator, I found I was becoming most fluent in Russian. We exchanged stories of our triumphs and failures, our moments of deep depression when animals died, our moments of joy when they successfully gave birth. We laughed a lot, toasted each other a lot and Lee and I fell in love with all of them, and I hope they felt the same about us. At the end of this marvellous meal, Spitzin (in spite of the fact that it was pitch dark, the temperatures below zero and that, as we had not unpacked, Lee and I were clad in thin clothing) insisted on taking us on a tour of the zoo by torchlight. As can be imagined, we saw very little and escaped pneumonia by a hair's breadth.

But now, at the end of our journey through the Soviet Union, we were to see the zoo in summer on a sunny day when all the leaves were glittering on the trees and Moscow was looking its best.

Spitzin produced, with a conjuror's flourish, a smart little pony and trap driven by a pretty young lady, and in this charming vehicle we conducted our tour of the zoo. It was indeed a triumphal royal tour such as I have never had in any other zoo in the world. We came to the spectacled bear cage, which was very exciting, for we had sent from Jersey one of the males that we had bred (the other went to Washington for the sake of detente) and now he in his turn had become a father and we could admire the lovely female cub (christened Lee, of course) cavorting about the cage. I am afraid that Lee (the bear) behaved very

Our long-awaited tour of the Moscow Zoo in a brightly painted pony and trap. It was a wonderful way of covering a lot of ground in a very short time and we managed to see nearly everything the zoo contained. And a most impressive collection of animals it is, all of them in beautiful condition, and lovingly watched over by a dedicated staff and their director, the incomparable Vladimir Spitzin.

The two magnificent cheetahs who objected strongly to our invasion of their privacy and obviously thought we were out to steal their lovely cubs. When the babies grow older they lose the curious mane of fur they have on their backs and necks.

badly, doing none of the things we wanted her to do and finally hanging upside down on the bars and urinating at the camera. Then we clopped off to see the cheetahs, two lovely females who occupied a large paddock containing (as well as their babies) some of the biggest four-leafed clovers I have ever seen. The mother cheetahs, not unnaturally, took a rather jaundiced view of this invasion of humanity into their tranquil lives, whereas their nine babies viewed the whole thing as rather fascinating, like a circus coming to town. We went into the paddock with them and the mothers put on a wonderful display of protective animosity. Ears flattened against their heads, eyes flashing, their lips drawn back to show their wonderful shining teeth, they hissed and spat at us and, when we ventured too close, did a wonderful warning 'dance'. Snarling and hissing, they would jump towards us in two leaps, their front legs hitting the ground with a loud thump each time. It was a very impressive demonstration of 'come this far and no further'. The babies were delightful, still with the extraordinary shock-headed mane they have when young, and the black 'tear' marks accentuating their lovely golden eyes. After the novelty of our existence had worn off, they left all the anti-human stuff to their mothers and proceeded to play hide-and-seek with each other, have wrestling matches, bite each other, chase bumble bees and do all the vital things it is necessary for a baby cheetah to do if it is to grow up to be a decent member of the felidae.

Our next stop was in a behind-the-scenes private world, a series of rooms stuffed with cages of frogs, toads and tortoises. After we had made suitable noises of appreciation at the tree frogs and watched the very rare spade-footed toads bury themselves as if by magic with the aid of a hard blade like an extension of the hind foot, we went into a

Left: *A member of the Moscow Zoo staff who has been there for forty-five years and whose speciality is the hand-rearing of young birds. One of her present charges is a steppe eagle still in its baby down.*

Below: *The walruses we visited were massive and seemed to suffer from chronic catarrh. Spitzin was most amused when I said that fascinating though they were, they would never win the Miss World contest.*

At one point in our tour Spitzin left the trap to re-appear shortly with two enchanting snow leopard cubs. Their fur was as soft as a dandelion clock, and their paws were enormous for their size. In spite of their youth, they still snarled at us in protest at being removed from their mother's side for only a few minutes.

special room where, in a large tank full of sea water, squatted Mathilda (who had been christened before they discovered it was a male), an octopus from the Sea of Japan with four-foot-long tentacles and soulful eyes. He did not mind being hauled out of his watery domain, and wrapped his tentacles round Lee and me in the most endearingly affectionate way, even though, from our point of view, it was a somewhat damp romance. However, when we lit the floodlights for filming, Mathilda did not like it and turned (in that wonderful iridescent way that octopuses do) from being pale cream with faint brown blotches to a fiery and infuriated brick-red, rolled his eyes indignantly at us, retreated behind his rocks and refused to cooperate.

After bidding a fond farewell to Mathilda we paused briefly to admire all the baby birds in a nursery, a strange melange of eaglets, owlets and ducklings, baby coots and young pheasants, and then proceeded on our way to a meeting I had been greatly looking forward to. In a huge pond lived two female walruses and, with the aid of a bucketful of odiferous fish, we got them to haul their huge bodies, wrinkled as the Michelin Man, out of the water so we could talk to them. They are so ungainly on land and yet, considering their bulk, so graceful in the water, it is quite extraordinary. They accepted fish from us with much bristling of whiskers, gnashing of their tusks and great snorts of enjoyment. As they both appeared to be suffering from chronic catarrh and did not have the benefit of handkerchiefs, the horrid results can be imagined rather than described. We left them making noises like a couple of elderly steam engines and hurried on to our next appointment. Here Spitzin left us in the pony and trap and reappeared a moment later, depositing in our laps two baby snow leopards, their fur as soft as wood ash, with huge eyes and fat paws. They lay in our arms, occasionally snarling and hissing at us in futile baby rage until we had filmed them and returned them to their mothers. So, with this joyous visit to the zoo, we brought our visit to the Soviet Union to an end, and what more fitting way to end than with friends and animals.

On the plane back to London we reviewed our lengthy journey. The conservation work being done in the Soviet Union had impressed us greatly. They give it an importance that few other countries in the world can boast and, though it is not perfect (no conservationist is ever satisfied), it is still of very high standard.

The nature reserves are numerous and enormous, and each that we saw seemed to be impeccably run by charming and devoted people with a deep interest in their jobs. There are, however, two points that — if our Soviet friends will forgive us — we would like to make. All the reserves are run by a variety of ministries and departments which, of course, makes for complications. The English proverb that too many cooks spoil the broth is a sound one and we think the whole magnificent reserve system in the Soviet Union would benefit tremendously from being answerable to only one central body. The other thing that worried us was that one reserve did not seem to know what another was doing, unless it was next door, as it were. We were constantly being asked what we had seen in other reserves and what their projects were. There did not seem to be (at least we could not discover one) any sort of regular news-sheet that could tell someone looking after musk ox what his counterpart was doing in the steppe for the saiga, or inform someone on Lake Baikal looking after sable what was being done for cormorants on the Volga. We are sure something of this sort would be extremely beneficial, for all the workers we met on the reserves evinced a deep interest and pride in their own conservation work, and wanted to know about the work of others as well. But these are minor criticisms. Suffice it to say that conservation is taken very seriously in the Soviet Union and we wish other countries in the world would treat it with the same respect.

Looking back on our travels my memories are rich and varied. I remember the gentle giant in Oka who gave me his coat because I admired it; I remember Natasha in her lovely cottage, telling us about her pets with twenty words of English and a wealth of mime; I remember the kindly brown wrinkled faces of the old ladies in the Tblisi market and how they would not let us pay for our purchases; I remember all the warmth and kindness we were shown. But above all, of course, I remember the wonderful animals we saw: the musk ox standing in their courageous ring, the Baikal seal rolling about on the ice and upstaging Lee, the sable's beautiful face swearing at us, the wonderful weasels in their desert home, the half-drowned badgers and foxes we rescued, red-breasted geese turning into the sun and the huge herd of saiga grazing across the sunset. I remember the pageant of flowers we saw, some so minute you had to get down on your knees to appreciate their beauty of form and colour.

All in all it was a magnificent and fascinating trip and we feel very privileged that the Soviet people allowed us to visit so many parts of their vast country and that everyone we met gave us unstintingly their warmth and affection.

I derive intense joy from meeting wild creatures in wild places. In return, I do what I can about those unique life forms that are about to disappear from our planet forever.

Twenty-five years ago I founded the Jersey Wildlife Preservation Trust. This organization studies endangered animal species, sets up breeding programmes in Jersey and then, when possible, introduces captive-bred specimens to the wild to boost declining natural populations. In addition, we work in the animal's country of origin, by assisting governments to train local personnel and construct breeding units and advising them on how to protect animals in their natural habitat.

If among these pages you have shared a little in my sense of privilege as a visitor to wild communities and you would like to help me in my efforts to save wildlife, then do write to me for details of our work and membership.

Gerald Durrell
Jersey

INDEX